The Harvest Festival

THE HARVEST FESTIVAL

FESTIVAL *A Play in*

Three Acts by SEAN O'CASEY

With a Foreword by Eileen O'Casey and an

Introduction by John O'Riordan THE NEW

YORK PUBLIC LIBRARY Astor, Lenox and

Tilden Foundations & READEX BOOKS 1979

FIRST EDITION

Copyright © 1979 The Estate of Sean O'Casey

The first impression of one thousand copies, set in Bembo type, with Bembo and Castellar display types, was printed on Mohawk Superfine paper at The Stinehour Press, Lunenburg, Vermont. It was designed by Marilan Lund.

Library of Congress Cataloging in Publication Data:

O'Casey, Sean, 1880–1964.
  The harvest festival.

  I. Title.
PR6029.C33H3 1979   822'.9'12   79–23318
ISBN 0–87104–273–8

Distributed by Readex Books, A Division of Readex Microprint Corporation

THE HARCOURT BRACE JOVANOVICH FUND
for Publications Based on Manuscripts in the
Berg Collection of English and American Literature
in The New York Public Library

Publication Number One

Contents

Clench Your Teeth

I THINK there is no better way to describe Sean's determination as a playwright than to quote from his own autobiography *Inishfallen, Fare Thee Well.*

It is some years ago, in fact many years have passed since Sean wrote "The Harvest Festival." It was sent to the Abbey Theatre, Dublin, in the hope of a production, about 1919.

"The Frost in the Flower" was the first play sent to the Abbey. This was returned with their saying "how interested they were in the play which was promising, but one of the main characters had been too critical, reminding them of various characters in Abbey plays. . . ."

Sean guessed this comment was wrong, and a little ridiculous, since he had been in the Abbey Theatre but twice and had seen only *Light* by Gogarty, *Androcles and the Lion* by Shaw, *The Jackdaw* by Lady Gregory, and another one-act play built on a short story by James Stephens. He had seen nothing in any of these that he could try to imitate.

Now "The Harvest Festival" was sent to the Abbey. The play brought back to Sean a letter saying that the work was well conceived, but badly executed; with an added note from Mr Lennox Robinson, then the Manager of the Abbey Theatre, saying that he liked very much the character of the clergyman in the play—which was something, but not enough for Sean.

There had been a good chance of the third play "The Crimson in the Tri-Colour" being produced, for Lady Gregory had written saying she was very interested in it; that it was evident that the author had something in him. But it could not be put on until the revolution was over, and it must be typed by the theatre, for no one could possibly attempt the reading of such written manuscript a second time. And then came a letter from Mr Robinson saying "that in moving from Clare Street to Foxrock, he had mislaid the play, and would Sean please furnish them with a copy." And Sean clenched his teeth, for there was no copy, not even notes from which a copy might be built. So his last state was as bad as his first.

There was nothing to do but forget, and go on; forget, and go on. He had made up his mind years ago that the Abbey Theatre curtain would go up on a play of his, and up it would go, sooner or later.

Yes, the Abbey Theatre curtain did go up on Sean's plays, in 1923 *The Shadow of a Gunman* and *Kathleen Listens In*, in 1924 *Juno and the Paycock* and *Nannie's Night Out*; 1926, *The Plough and the Stars*.

So I am pleased that The New York Public Library is publishing this play as Sean wrote it. The play was in a chest among other papers all the years of our married life; I don't think Sean ever really wanted it printed, he had developed so much; this work was behind him. Writers on Sean's work have said all there is to say as to the characters in "The Harvest Festival" coming to light in later plays, *Red Roses for Me*, *The Drums of Father Ned*, and *The Bishop's Bonfire*.

When reading this play students of drama will see the seeds of Sean's later works. I hope also this short preface will say—if you truly believe in yourself in any talent you may have "first decide slowly and deeply whether it is in you to do a thing; if you decide that you can, then do it, even though it kept you busy until the very last hour of life"—clench your teeth, and keep on.

EILEEN O'CASEY
(*Mrs Sean O'Casey*)

Introduction

BEFORE the success of the Abbey Theatre's production of Sean
O'Casey's first produced play, *The Shadow of a Gunman* (1923),
and the outstanding triumph the following year of his *Juno and the
Paycock*, O'Casey as a labourer had written several early, unproduced
plays; plays which in his later years as a supremely acknowledged inter-
national dramatist he was inclined to regard as fledgling, apprentice
work. These early attempts at playwriting were originally offered to
the Abbey Theatre between 1919 and 1921; rejected for various drama-
turgic but not (on hindsight) wholly justifiably artistic reasons; and,
though the Playwright never made any other attempts to market or
publish them, all of them—with the now sole exception of "The Harvest Festival"—have since unfortunately sunk into the limbo of forgotten achievements, the manuscripts having disappeared without trace. As
far as we know, "The Harvest Festival" is the only play to survive
among those early efforts, which included "The Frost in the Flower"
and "The Crimson in the Tri-Colour."

During the stage success of *Juno and the Paycock* in London in 1926,
O'Casey told one newspaper interviewer that whilst he was "pounding
the Abbey Theatre, in Dublin, with manuscripts," he fell into a queue
each day to draw the dole. He was working at nearly all kinds of jobs,
even road making. But from the human beings he worked with he got
the life he has since put into his work. "I was on strike with them. I
starved with them, and I looked for jobs with them." His first efforts
at playwriting resulted mainly from his association with the St Laurence
O'Toole National Club, whose activities included "hurling, football
and amateur theatricals."

The Irish historian R. M. Fox, in an article entitled "Portrait of
O'Casey as a Young Man,"[1] recalls that whilst O'Casey was managing
the small social club at Dublin's Liberty Hall organised by Delia Larkin,
sister to the renowned Jim Larkin (1876–1947)—the widely revered

---

1 *The Sting & the Twinkle: Conversations with Sean O'Casey* ed E. H. Mikhail and John
O'Riordan (London: Macmillan 1974) 13–15.

Irish Labour leader—he had written "a strike play" for Liberty Hall (the Transport Union headquarters) dealing with 1913, the year of industrial turmoil. But he told Fox he had then "never done any professional writing for the theatre." The play in question was, undoubtedly, "The Harvest Festival," which O'Casey later submitted as his second play to the Abbey Theatre Directorate.

"The Harvest Festival," O'Casey tells us, in a passage in his fourth book of Autobiography, *Inishfallen, Fare Thee Well*,

dealt with the efforts of militant members of the unskilled unions to put more of the fibre of resistance to evil conditions of pay and life into the hearts and minds of the members of the craft unions whose gospel was that what was good enough for the fathers was good enough for the sons. The action took place in the busy preparations made by a church for holding the annual harvest festival, which the Anglo-catholics sneeringly called the Feast of Saint Pumpkin and all Vegetables.

The play was not considered suitable for production in the judgement of the Abbey directors, who included W. B. Yeats and Lady Gregory, along with Lennox Robinson as their Theatrical Manager. The original manuscript, written in O'Casey's closely inscribed handwriting, was found among the Playwright's papers at the time of his death in 1964 and subsequently sold to the New York Public Library's Berg Collection in 1969. The discovery of what is undoubtedly the earliest O'Casey play we have in existence, dating from approximately 1918–19 and written in the Playwright's naturalistic manner, is clearly an exciting and memorable event. But we must not forget that it was never either produced or published during Sean O'Casey's lifetime, nor are there any indications that he would have wished it otherwise. In her Preface Mrs O'Casey has told of Sean's reaction to the Abbey Theatre's criticism. The full text of the Abbey comment on both "The Frost in the Flower" and "The Harvest Festival"—enshrined in a letter dated 26 January 1920—appears in print for the first time in the recently published *Letters of Sean O'Casey*,[2] edited by Dr David Krause:

[Of "The Harvest Festival"]: This play is interestingly conceived but not well executed. It is seldom dramatic and many of the characters suffer from being too typical of their class or profession (Williamson, Sir J. Vane, for instance).

2 Volume 1 (1910–1941) [New York: Macmillan 1975] 91–92.

They are conventional conceptions, as unreal as the "Stage Irishman" of 20 years ago. If the author has got these typical figures firmly planted in his imagination we should advise him to try to replace them by figures drawn as accurately as possible from his own experience.

[Next follows a critique of "The Frost in the Flower."]

We are sorry to return these plays for the author's work interests us, but we don't think either would succeed on the stage.

On dramatic grounds alone, much of this criticism can be challenged, and while nobody would claim there is a rambunctious character in the play comparable with, for example, either "Captain" Boyle or Joxer Daly, or even Fluther Good or Bessie Burgess, the play has a distinct lineage with O'Casey's later plays—*Red Roses for Me*, *The Star Turns Red*, and *The Drums of Father Ned*. One must concede, however, that much of the richly worded, zany dialogue so characteristic of the maturer O'Casey is missing. Some of the characters have their counterparts in later O'Casey characters. Melville Williamson, for example, has overtones of Adolphus Grigson in *The Shadow of a Gunman*. The labourers, Jack and Tom, share affinities with the workmen in *The Bishop's Bonfire*; and the character of the clergyman, the Rev J. Jennings, is clearly an earlier model for the Rev E. Clinton, who appears in *Red Roses for Me*.

The factions that take place between the Rector and his Select Vestry parallel those described by O'Casey in the pages of his Autobiography *Pictures in the Hallway*, in the chapter "The Sword of Light." Undeniably, too, there is a good deal of self-portraiture in the main character of Jack Rocliffe, who, in turn, is a prototype of Ayamonn Breydon, the hero of *Red Roses for Me*. There are traces, also, of O'Casey's friend of earlier days, the Tram Conductor, in Tom Nimmo—with his humorous catchphrases and asides, such as, "Protestants is curious animals." O'Casey later expands the device more skilfully in his familiar trio of plays—*The Shadow of a Gunman*, *Juno and the Paycock*, and *The Plough and the Stars*—notably in the characters of Shields, Grigson, Boyle, Joxer, the Covey, and Fluther.

The objection will no doubt be made that the play is too loosely knit and too tightly packed with the Playwright's radical opinions. Such criticism could also be levelled at Shaw's plays, skin-tight as many of these are with opinions that are both jaundiced and jocular. It is noteworthy that Bertolt Brecht, commenting on one occasion on Shaw's technique, might almost have been analysing O'Casey's own methods, when he reflected: "His world is one that arises from opinions. The opinions of his characters constitute their fates. Shaw creates a play by inventing a series of complications which give his characters a chance to develop their opinions as fully as possible and to oppose them to our own—."[3] Those who regard opinions in plays as damned spots, O'Casey once wrote, are "proud and haughty." And he went on to recall: " 'A playwright has nothing to do with opinions,' said W. B. Yeats vehemently in my bothered ear once, failing to realise himself that this very declaration was one of the oddest opinions among the multitude showered down on the world of man."[4]

It is not too fanciful to suggest that O'Casey, like Shaw, saw himself from the very beginning in terms of a theatrical terrorist (or "a holy terror," as they say in some parts of Ireland), tempering his extremist views with weapons of raillery and laughter. He uses these weapons to a marked degree in "The Harvest Festival." His is also the humour of tragicomedy—the muse he forever courted—with a perpetual conflict between contraries, as in Blake ("Excess of sorrow laughs. Excess of Joy weeps"). And though, undeniably, the characters in "The Harvest Festival" are less gifted oratorically than those of their successors—beginning with *The Shadow of a Gunman* right the way through to *The Drums of Father Ned*—, nevertheless, as is evident in "The Harvest Festival" itself, the language is still tuppence-coloured rather than penny-plain. And, as in Shaw, there is plenty of hard, thumping talk.

Although "The Harvest Festival" lays no claim to greatness, historical reasons alone dictate that it should be published and included in the corpus of O'Casey's works. The present justification, too, for its long-delayed yet eagerly awaited publication may in some measure be attributed to the rueful comment O'Casey was later to make on his early, rejected plays with the rejoinder:

It was years after, when he had left Ireland forever, that bitterness, mingled with scorn, overtook him, for he began to realize that the plays refused by the Abbey Theatre were a lot better than many they had welcomed, and had played on to the stage with drums and colours.

Here, then, without any such pomp or pageantry, but with the appraisal and blessing of the Playwright's widow, Eileen O'Casey, and

3 *Brecht on Theatre* ed John Willet (London: Eyre Methuen 1973) 11.
4 *Under a Colored Cap* (London: Macmillan 1963) 254.

approval of The New York Public Library, "The Harvest Festival" appears in print in its own right and in its original version for the first time. The springtime of the dramatist's Dublin life will not, therefore, have been forgotten, as all the wheat will have been gathered into the one granary in preparation for the harvest centenary celebrations of the Playwright's birth that will be celebrated throughout the world in 1980.

JOHN O'RIORDAN

Act 2. Continued.

Jack: Good evening, Mrs Duffy: I haven't a moment to spare, mother. Things are getting lively. They have called out the troops. Some of our Leaders were arrested to-day. Many of the strikers have been injured, and hundreds are being arrested. A cargo of scabs come over from England tomorrow; may God help any of them that fall into the clutches of the men — never mind whats' in the pot, mother; I've not time to wait — a cup of tea will do well.

Mrs Rocliffe: — You'll be killin' yourself runnin' about like this, an' not takin' time to eat a bit. But, sure, you might as well be talkin' to the wall.

(She fills out Jacks' tea, which he takes rapidly; as he takes his tea, he occasionally writes in a notebook which he places beside him on the table)

Mrs Duffy. Do you think it 'ill soon be over, Jack.

Jack: (enthusiastically) It's going to be a bitter, venomous struggle. The men are more determined than they ever were to gain recognition of their Union. Not that I, personally, care a damn about that. I am not so eager that the men should take some of the power out of the employers hands as I am that they should take the men should take the whole power into their own; I'm not so eager that the men should gain the right towards a living wage as I'm that they should overthrow the wage-system altogether. But the time for that is not yet. The Leaders of Labour are as yet like children that have been born out of due season. Sometimes the rank and file are ahead of the Leaders; Sometimes the Leaders are ahead of the rank and file. When the advanced thought of the Leaders is fused with the advanced action of the men — then will come the Revolution. But I'm talking foolishly, Mrs Duffy, for wisdom consists not in talking of what I understand myself, but in talking of what everybody else understands as well.

Mrs Duffy: Faith, an' you're talkin' greek to me, Jack.

Jack: The building trade is out today. It's splendid to see the men, to be with them, to be one in fight for human freedom. This fight will go down in History. At last in Ireland the workers have begun to knit the first strands of the Red Cap, which is the only crown for the head of Granuaile.

Mrs Duffy: Here's somebody else comin' up the stairs now.

(They all listen)

A knock at the door on right, at which Mrs Rocliffe springs up from where she has been sitting at the fire, and, running across the room, opens the door

Mrs R. It's th' Rector. Come in, sir, come in. Jack is just

The Harvest Festival
A Play in Three Acts

Cast

REV J. JENNINGS	Rector of St Brendan's
REV W. BISHOPSON	Curate of St Brendan's
MELVILLE WILLIAMSON	a Churchwarden
SIR JOCELYN VANE	a Synodsman and leading man of commerce
JACK ROCLIFFE*	a Labourer; afterwards on strike
TOM NIMMO*	a Bricklayer
BILL BROPHY	a Docker on strike
SIMON WAUGH	Sexton of St Brendan's
MRS WILLIAMSON	
CLARICE	Her daughter
MRS ROCLIFFE	Jack's mother
MRS DUFFY	a Poor Parishioner

Time: The Present
The first act takes place on Monday, the second on the Friday and the third on the Sunday of the same week.

Act One. Scene: The Drawing-Room of the Williamsons
Act Two. Scene: The Tenement Home of the Rocliffes
Act Three. Scene: The Exterior of St Brendan's Church.

S. Ō CATHASAIGH
18, Abercorn Road.
Dublin

* In the revision of Act 1 (Appendix), O'Casey was experimenting with different names for these characters—see the notes to pages 67.26, 67.28, 83.7, and 84.1.

Act One

Scene: The parlour or sitting-room of the Williamsons: it is furnished not so much to ensure the comfort, or to demonstrate the refined tastes of the Williamsons, but, rather to impress those who may be visitors with a sense of the family dignity in the plenitude of household goods. Everything is as big, as vivid and as glaring as possible. Pictures crowd together on the walls (which are painted from the skirting halfway up a brilliant crimson, & from that to the ceiling an equally brilliant yellow) interspersed with such Scriptural mottoes as: "God is Love," "Watch and Pray," "All Ye Works of the Lord: Bless Ye the Lord." The doors—one of which is on the left side of stage, and the other at back on the right—are painted in sky-blue panels and cream borders. A Bow-window, shrouded in white curtains, is at back of stage on left side. Between this window and the door on right is a piano, over which is a boldly lettered motto: "Sing Praises unto the Lord."

On one side of the window is a pink delph pedestal on which is a green delph flowerpot containing an artificial plant; on the other side of the window are the same ornaments with the colours reversed—a green pedestal and pink pot. Loudly upholstered chairs are sprinkled about the room, and a lounge is sprawling between the door on right and fireplace. A table covered with a crimson cloth has been drawn back from the centre of the rooms towards the left, on the table is a huge family Bible.

The fireplace is on the extreme right, and its furnishings are of polished brass.

The floor is covered with a gaudily coloured carpet, and a white hair rug, which has been stretched before the fire, is thrown upon the lounge. At present newspapers cover the furniture nearest the fireplace. A marble clock, surrounded by imposing vases, ticks proudly on the mantle shelf.

Tom Nimmo is discovered putting in fancy tiles in the hearth before the fireplace. He is bent down over his work.

Mrs Williamson is standing beside him watching as he works. She is a fairly stout woman of about forty, dressed in a sober dress of solemn black vulgarly decorated with purple trimmings. She evidently affects a simplicity with which her natural sympathies are not in accord. She wears a wristlet watch; bangles encircle her wrist, and a long many looped necklace of beads encircles her neck and dangles down below her bosom. Her face is harsh & proud, and, her whole manner of obtrusive & affected simplicity indicates that she considers herself far above the ordinary and sin-loving mortals with whom she lives & has her being. She is watching Tom as he taps a tile gently here and there or places a small straight edge over his work to see that it is level. As she watches Tom she sings in thin but decided tones the refrain of a hymn.

> *"In the sweet Bye and Bye.*
> *We shall meet on that beautiful shore;*
> *In the sweet bye and bye*
> *We shall meet on that beautiful shore."*

[MRS WILLIAMSON]
What do you put that little bit of wood over the tiles for?

TOM
Thats a straight edge, ma'am; it shows whether the tiles is right and level.

MRS WILLIAMSON
How wonderful! That's a lovely idea for my Sunday School Class next Sunday! The Christian's Straight-Edge that is the Straight Edge that makes us feel the roughness and unevenness of sin; what is it that reveals the ridges and hollows of the sinful heart; that makes us feel so happy when we know our lives have been lived in a smooth level of righteousness—what is it?

TOM
God! I'm sure I don't know, ma'am.

MRS WILLIAMSON
The Book, the Book, the Bible. That is the Straight-Edge that—
(*A loud sound of an electric bell is heard.*)
I'm sure that['s] Mr Bishopson our new curate and Clarice coming

back from decorating the church. I'll have to leave you for a few minutes.

(*She goes out by door on right at back; when she reaches the door, and as she is going out she pauses to shout:*)

Go on with your work, Maggie, I'll open it myself.

TOM

(*alone, mimicing*)

I'll have to leave you for a few minutes. Begor it's a pity that you'd ever come back. The new curate and Clarice comin' back from decoratin' the church for the Harvest Festival. Damn her and her Harvest Festival, an' I dyin' for a smoke.

(*He takes a clay pipe from his pocket & proceeds to enjoy a smoke.*)

I'm beginnin' to think she's not all there when she starts talkin' about puttin' straight-edges on peoples' hearts. It must be a curious family. I'd rather oul' Williamson was tied to her than me. Damn it, she never took her eyes off me since I came into the room to do this bit of a job. Protestants is curious animals. There's Jack one, that never goes to church an' says he doesn't believe in prayer, & there's this oul' one I suppose never out o' church—except when she's watchin' people,—an' never done prayin' an' singin' hymns. An' then there's some Protestan' clergyman that make themselves look as like a priest as possible, & there's others that kill themselves tryin' to look as unlike priests as possible. An' Jack tells me there's clergymen preach that the Protestant Church'll never get on till it becomes more Protestan' than it is, an' others preachin' that it'll never get on till it becomes more Catholic than it is; an' some clergymen say that the Cross should be over every church, & others sayin' that it should be over none; an' some say, accordin' to Jack, that St Patrick was a Protestant, an' others that he was a Catholic, an' others again, that he was neither a Catholic nor a Protestant, an' Jack says he doesn't believe such a man ever existed, or that there must have been six or seven St Patricks, an' even if it was true, that it is a pity he ever came to Ireland, for we'd have been happier without him. Be heavens, I can't understand them at all, for if—

5

(The door on right back opens and Mrs Williamson re-enters carrying a number of huge heads of cabbage. Tom excitedly pulls the pipe out of his mouth, puts it into his pocket and resumes his work at the tiles.)

MRS WILLIAMSON

What do you think of these, Mr Workman? Ar[e]n't they just lovely! It would be hard to get the like of them in a shop.

TOM

Them is grand cabbages. One of them 'ud make a dinner for a navvy's family. Was it yourself that grew them, ma'am?

MRS WILLIAMSON

Oh! dear no; thank God we are able to buy everything we want. These have been sent up from the country by a friend of ours for the Harvest Festival. Wouldn't they look splendid, now around the pulpit, or put somewhere in the chancel where everybody could see them.

TOM

You're jokin' ma'm; they'd look better smokin' on a dish makin' a fine collar for a pig's cheek. It's a curious look a church 'ud have with cabbages knockin' about in it.

MRS WILLIAMSON

You think that, poor man, because you cannot understand. You look at it from a Roman Catholic point of view, I suppose, an' were never at a Harvest Festival.

TOM

Never, ma'am in a church, though I was several times at a Harvest Home in the country; but that was always held in a barn with plenty of singin' an' dancin' an' lashin's of drink.

MRS WILLIAMSON

What a terrible way of thanking God by committing sin. Thank God, we know better than that. We bring our offerings to the church. Grapes and apples, cabbages, potatoes, turnips, parsnips, melons, bread, an' sprigs of corn, rye an' wheat, an' with these before our eyes, we give thanks to the Giver of all for the "kindly fruits of the earth" in prayer an' psalm singing.

(*Mrs Williamson goes over to the table and removing the ornaments that are there, arranges the cabbages around the family Bible.*)

TOM

(*To himself*)

Well, it seems all right to see priests an' altar boys movin' about between candles and pictures an' images, but it 'ud be a comical sight to see them walkin' between rows of cabbages an' heaps of potatoes, & to feel in the church instead of the scent of incense, the smell of celery, parsley an' thyme. I heard that Cromwell turned churches into stables, but it beats all to think of them turnin' churches into market gardens. God save us but Protestants is curious animals.

MRS WILLIAMSON

Isn't this a terrible strike that's going on at present. I pity the poor foolish ignorant men, though it's almost a sin to pity them. Mr Williamson is very anxious for fear that his men should be drawn into it, but I don't think there's any danger of that, do you?

TOM

There's every danger of it, ma'am. The men is gone mad with the Socialist preachin' that's bein' spouted everywhere of late years. I hope to God it won't spread to us.

MRS WILLIAMSON

That would be terrible. When will the poor ignorant workmen get common-sense, and realise that God intended that they should be content to do the work that come to their hands. Oh, if they only knew the blessedness of content, & a quiet trust in God they would never trouble their heads about a strike. Oh, if they would only become converted and think only of that beautiful home that awaits all those that suffer patiently the few passing tribulations of this world: (*She sings*)

7

Oh, think of the home over there,
By the side of the river of light,
Where the Saints all immortal and fair
Are robed in their garments of white.
Over there ———. Over there!
Oh, think of the home over there!
Over there ———. Over there!
Oh, think of the home over there.

Oh think of the friends over there
Who before us the journey have trod,
Oh the songs that they breathe on the air,
In their home———

(*The hall-door bell again rings violently.*)
My goodness there they are now, Mr Bishopson and Clarice.
(*She hurries out.*)

TOM

The divil speed you. She watches you so closely that she won't let you try to straighten your back. I wonder is it worth while to try to get a few pulls. I'll chance it, if it's the Curate and Clarice she won't be back for a few minutes. (*He imitates her song*)
"Over there ——— Over there
Oh, think of the home there"
It's thinkin' I am that it gives me enough to do to think of the home over here. Bad an' all as it is what will it be like in a few weeks if we're called out in this cursed strike. It's easy for Jack to crow over it, he hasn't eight children and a wife to feed. If he had, maybe, he wouldn't be so anxious to be goin' about half-mad with hunger an' anxiety listenin' to Labour Leaders roarin' at you that you were fightin' a battle for freedom and a better life. We never had a bit of peace since Jack come to the job. He's always stirrin' up the men with his talk of why shouldn't the workers go in motor cars, and their wives wear silks an' satins like the rich. An' when you tell him we can't all ride in motor-cars, he'll tell you then we should all walk. Damn it all couldn't we be worse off; can't we

take a penny tram now an' again an' what more do we want. I wish to God these agitators would leave well enough alone. It's us poor divils that want to plod along in peace that suffer. The employers persecute us if we are loyal to the Trades' Union; the Union persecutes us if we are loyal to the employers. We are slaves at work, slaves in our Union and slaves at home. If we come out on strike the police try to bludgeon us; if we stop in the strikers try to bludgeon us, & we are of all men the most miserable. Let them go out that wants to go, I don't. It's a shame to drag a man into anything he wants to keep out of.

(*The door at the back of stage on right opens and Jack Rocliffe enters with a sweeping brush in his hand. He is a well-developed working man of about twenty-five years of age. His face is boldly formed, and heavy eyebrows give strength and vigour to gentle and thoughtful eyes. He is dressed carelessly, but more neatly than the average labourer. He has a crimson scarf around his neck, and wears a brown jersey and white moleskin trousers. A dark green soft hat covers his head. He speaks earnestly, which at times is changed into a humourous cynicism. As Jack enters Tom violently snatches the pipe out of his mouth, lets it slip from his hands, makes a frantic effort to save it, but fails & the clay pipe smashes on the hearth.*)

TOM

Why the hell don't you whistle when you're comin' in; there's the pipe bruck, now. I thought you were that oul' rip comin' in again.

JACK

Oh, is she gone at last? What singular inducement prompted her to leave your sweet society?

TOM

There was a knock. The new curate & Miss Clarice home again from decoratin' the church for her bloody Harvest Festival.

JACK

If this strike develops much more there will be a Harvest Festival in Dublin, in which the Labour Leaders will be the clergy, the strikers the congregation; in which curses will be prayers, hymns

9

will be lamentations, the choir will be police and soldiers, the seed will be the blood of the proletariat, and the crop will be the conception of the New Idea of Labour in Ireland.

TOM

The curse of God on the strike. What good will it do me or me wife and children, only, maybe, starve us to death?

JACK

It will kill you or cure you, and either change will mean added strength to the Cause of Labour. A slave yourself, you will probably beget slaves, and if the workers are content to remain slaves, then, as Emerson says, it is but the case of any other vermin—the more there are the worse for Labour.

TOM

And this is the glorious Brotherhood about which you are always preachin'.

JACK

No Brotherhood can exist between you and me. You are a link in the chain that fetters me, & the sooner you are smashed to pieces the sooner I shall be free.

TOM

And you call the employers beasts, an' what in the name of God are you?

JACK

A claw in the foot and a fang in the mouth of the great Beast of Labour. But such as you are a muzzle on Labour's mouth, and a sheathe on its claw, so that we are rent and cannot rend again; are torn asunder and cannot injure the power that destroys us.

TOM

I'm glad that I know what charity is; & that I ought to love my neighbour. Here, hand us that straightedge, till we get out of this place—that blasted oul' one may be back any minute.

JACK

Evidently, Tom, you are too good to be trusted alone in the room.
She is probably afraid you would steal the Bible.

TOM

She'll wait a long time before I'd be bothered with her Bible.

JACK

She doesn't know you, Tom, so well as you know yourself. What
do you care about Bibles or Prayerbooks?

TOM

I said nothing about Prayerbooks; them is different.

JACK

And just as valueless. Do you know Swinburne, Tom?

TOM

Swinburne? Is he a brickie or a plumber?

JACK

Neither, you poor unenlightened soul—he's a poet.

TOM

What the Hell do I know about poets!

JACK

Just about as much as you want to know about Bibles or Prayer-
books. You should read Swinburne, Tom; it would do you good.
Poor Tom, you suffer under a dual tyranny—afraid of your soul in
the next world and afraid of your body in this. Was it not John
Mitchel who said "the Irish people would be free long ago only
for their damned souls"; well, the workers would be free long ago
only for their damned bodies.

(*The door on right at back opens, and Mrs Williamson, who has two
huge turnips and a bunch of carrots in her arms—followed by the Rev
Mr Bishopson and Clarice, enters.*)

MRS WILLIAMSON

Now aren't they just gorgeous Mr Bishopson. They're the loveliest
turnips I have ever seen, don't you think so Mr Bishopson?

MR BISHOPSON

(*Bishopson is a small sandyhaired man of about thirty. He is greatly gathered up in the shoulders, & his head is thrust forward in such a way as almost to amount to a deformity. He has a peculiar habit before he begins to speak of trying to get [his] head back where it ought to be. And when he has spoken, of trying to thrust it more forwardly than ever.*)

They are certainly beauties, Mrs Williamson, beauties. They should prove a source of great attraction in the church.

(*Mrs Williamson arranges the turnips and the carrots on the table beside the cabbages, & the three stand back as if a more distant view would enhance their look.*)

JACK
to Tom
Distance lends enchantment to the view.

TOM
Ssh. They'll hear you.

MRS WILLIAMSON
I wonder where ought we to put them.

JACK
In a pot ma-am, to be cooked for some half starved family.

MR BISHOPSON
Who is this fellow?

CLARICE
That's one of father's workmen; father says he's a very impudent fellow.

MR BISHOPSON
Is he a Protestant?

CLARICE
He was, but father says he never goes to church now.

MR BISHOPSON
If he was a Protestant he'd know his place—(*to Jack*)—we did not

ask you for your opinion my good man. (*With great dignity*) It is more fitting for you to mind your work, and do your duty in that state of life into which it has pleased God to call you.

MRS WILLIAMSON

When our circumstances are humble our conduct must be humble also.

JACK

Allow me to point out, sir, that you have quoted the Cathecism incorrectly. The phrase is not, in that state of life unto which it has pleased God to call you, but in that state of life unto which it shall please God to call you. And believe me that I believe that God has called me to fight the oppression with which the poor are oppressed, and not only that, but I have pleased myself to believe that there is no thanksgiving in the decoration of your churches with corn and fruit and vegetables while one man or woman or child, ay, or beast in the field or bird in the air is hungry. By thanking God for the comfort of a few we are ignorantly cursing him for the misery of the many. And I am also called to believe that, though we all may not be called to be equally wise, we are all called to be equally happy. And as it is the content of the few that makes the world presently miserable, so it will [be] the discontent of the many that will make the world ultimately happy.

CLARICE

I suppose you know, sir, that you are talking to a clergyman.

MR BISHOPSON

Pray, be calm my dear Miss Williamson.

CLARICE

Oh, how can I be calm when I remember what I saw when we were coming home: a crowd of drunken fellows like you in spite of the police, pushing a car laden with flour and a poor horse over the Quay wall into the river. Oh, mother if you were to see the struggles of the poor horse in the water; I shall never forget it.

13

MRS WILLIAMSON
And what happen'd to the poor driver?

MR BISHOPSON
After a severe struggle the police managed to save him. It was delightful to see the way they punished the cowardly wretches. A number of them had to be brought to hospital. (*To Jack*) I suppose if you had been there you would have helped in the glorious work of killing the man and drowning the horse.

JACK
Had I been there I would have endeavoured to save the horse.

MR BISHOPSON
All about the horse and nothing about the man.

JACK
Let your condemnation fall upon the employers of labour, sir, who mourn for the loss of their horses, and laugh at the loss of men.

TOM
We're done here, now, Mrs Williamson.

MRS WILLIAMSON
Then off you go down to the kitchen and settle the range there. Come, Mr Bishopson, never mind those who are dead in their sins, & know not nor understand the Peace of the Gospel.

MR BISHOPSON
My dear Mrs Williamson it is our priviledge to awake those who are dead in trespasses and sins, & to teach them to submit themselves to all their governors, teachers, spiritual pastors and masters—

JACK
Meaning the employers of course.

⎰ CLARICE   For shame to interrupt a clergyman!
⎱ MRS WILLIAMSON   Shocking pride and want of manners.

MR BISHOPSON
Ignorance, my dear ladies, ignorance. As I was about to say as well

that is the duty of the church to teach the masses to order themselves lowly and reverently to all their betters—

JACK

Meaning you and the ladies, of course.

MR BISHOPSON

Meaning me and the ladies, and (*bowing to Mrs Williamson*) Mr Williamson, of course, and not only us but even that man beside you, for he is a tradesman while you are simply a common labouring man.

JACK

There you are, Tom, bow your acknowledgement of such a disinterested and gracious tribute to your superiority over me. Bow, you poor slave, lowly and reverently to your betters here who recognize you to be a great deal less than they but something more than I.

TOM

Don't be bringin' me into it; I have said nothing an' I want to say nothing, good, bad or indifferent.

MRS WILLIAMSON

There's a good, sweet man that knows his place.

CLARICE

I wish father was here and the other would quickly know his place, too.

JACK

Allow me to assure you I am sorry if I have offended you. None of you seems to know that there are two types of workers. The one an old poisonous growth of what is called the Capitalistic System, the other a new vigorous growth that is rapidly extinguishing the older one; the one satisfied with the least that the employing-class will give; the other dissatisfied with the most the employing-class can bestow; the one content to remain a slave, the other determined to become a man; the one afraid to eat of the tree of knowl-

15

edge, the other climbing the tree for the fruit of the topmost branches; the one anxious lest anyone should hear him speak, the other eager that everybody should listen to him; the one willing to submit to any kind of life to avoid death, the other prepared to meet any form of death that he may have life. Tom is the one type and I am the other.

MR BISHOPSON

I have been told you are a Protestant, and if you are, then, what you have said forces me to say that you are a disgrace to the Protestant Church of Ireland.

JACK

You have made, sir, a sensible statement at last, and I beg to be allowed to exemplify it. Every Protestant that lives in a one-room tenement is a disgrace to the Church; every protestant that rots in a Sanatorium is a disgrace to the Church; every Protestant whose life is a constant, deadly struggle with Poverty is a disgrace to the Church; every ill-clad, hungry Protestant man, woman or child is a disgrace to the Church. While the Church is busy moulding us for Heaven, the world is busy helping us on towards the hospital, the asylum, the jail or the workhouse.

TOM

Come on, Jack, down to the kitchen till we settle the range.

MR BISHOPSON

You don't look very hungry, my good man, and you are fairly well-dressed—for a labourer.

JACK

Too well-dressed, perhaps, in your opinion, sir. But I am proud of my class, the workers—

"Men my brothers, men the workers, ever reaping something new,
    That which they have done but earnest of the things that they shall do."

But well-dressed as I am, & well fed as I appear to be, I have shared the workers' shame. After my father died, when I was but five years of age, I lived for ten years on a cup of tea & a few cuts of dry bread daily, with a few potatoes on Sunday in honour of the Christian Festival, and becoming sickly and delicate on the dainty food I was receiving, charitable people took pity on me and gave me bottles of medicine to give me an appetite. I have heard that Dante was pointed out as "the man who had been in Hell," but there are thousands of souls in this country who are never out of it.

(*During this discussion between Bishopson and Jack, Mrs Williamson has been arranging and admiring the heap of vegetables on the table, singing in a low but perfectly audible voice the following stanzas of a hymn:*

"Let us gather up the sunbeams lying all around our path;
Let us keep the wheat and roses, casting out the thorns and chaff;
Let us find our dearest comforts in the blessings of today,
With a patient hand removing all the briars from the way.
    Then scatter seeds of kindness, then scatter seeds of kindness
Then scatter seeds of kindness for our reaping by an' by!"

(*Clarice stands beside the curate with her hand on his arm, as if to draw him away, and Tom is at door on right at back, which he opens as if to go out, and shuts it again to appeal to Jack to come on to settle the range below.*)

MR BISHOPSON
I don't believe your story; it is impossible; the conditions you brag about would kill any child.

JACK
It certainly kills the most of them; but some—

MRS WILLIAMSON
(*Coming forward*)
I really cannot permit you to suffer this insolence any longer, my dear Mr Bishopson; Clarice dear, bring Mr Bishopson down to the garden, & get him to help you pluck some chrysanthe[m]ums for

17

the church. And you, sir, go on down to your work at once. And, remember, I shall certainly [speak] about you to Mr Williamson the moment he returns.

CLARICE

If you don't, I certainly will, Mama. Come along into the garden, Mr Bishopson.

(*Clarice trips saucily out by door at left, followed by Mr Bishopson.*)

MRS WILLIAMSON

Now, then Mr Trade[s]man, bring this impudent fellow down to his work.

(*Tom gathers up his tools, and is going towards door on right, at back, when it opens, & Mr Melville Williamson enters.*)

WILLIAMSON

My God, Nimmo, are you not done here yet?

TOM

Just done, now, sir.

WILLIAMSON

(*With a shout*)

Then get down to the other job, will you. You're not on strike yet, are you?

TOM

Oh, no sir, not yet, sir.

(*He hurriedly departs by door on right. Mr Williamson watches Jack as he slowly follows Tom out by door on right.*)

WILLIAMSON

By God, I'll settle you soon, my boy; wait till this strike is settled, and we'll soon pack you off about your business.

(*Williamson is about fifty-five years of age, and is becoming very stout, due, no doubt, to an easy time enjoyed since his promotion as senior Foreman. He apes his employers in his manners and in his dress. He is obsequious to those above him, and savage to those above whom he has risen.*

18

He is destitute of all intelligence outside of that necessary to understand his work, and which has been acquired by long practice. As Churchwarden his dignity has expanded into a fuller importance. He demonstrates his lively sense of this by adding numerous pendants to his watchchain; by wearing on his fingers a number of rings; by wearing clothes of a fashionable cut & by adopting a toilet of tall collars and [white] shirt[s] which make him essentially uncomfortable. He has a large, wide, heavy face, a vulgar mouth, a high forehead, caused, not by thought or study, but by the disappearance of hair on the front of his head. He bears himself as if he thought the position of Churchwarden conferred upon him a first-class seat in the senate of heaven. He goes to church, not because he believes there is any necessity for such a course of conduct, but because he thinks it essential for the good of others that he should be there. He is astounded at the idea of any parishioner being absent when he deigns to be present. His name appears in the various Parochial subscription lists, for he argues that if you can't purchase paradise, a churchwarden must have a good name there.

He walks over to the fireplace, which Mrs Williamson is re-arranging, looks at the hearth, & then goes over to the table on which are the vegetables.)

WILLIAMSON

Who the hell put these things on the table? Do you hear me asking a question Mrs Williamson? (*Raising his voice*) Are you damn well deaf Mrs Williamson?

MRS WILLIAMSON

"I hear you calling me."

MR WILLIAMSON

Look here, I've had enough of your sarcastic answers. Who put these things on the table?

MRS WILLIAMSON

Maybe, my dear love, they grew there.

WILLIAMSON

(*Fiercely flinging them onto the floor*)

19

Let them grow somewhere else, then. Where did you put the books I left here? Do you hear me talking to you?

MRS WILLIAMSON

Don't you think if you opened your eyes a little you might find them.

WILLIAMSON

(*Walking over to her, and catching her by the arms*)
You will make me lose my temper, will you. Do you want me to knock you down?

MRS WILLIAMSON

Whether I wish that or not, I'm sure you would like to do it. Ever since I married you I am hourly expecting that demonstration of affection, dear.

MR WILLIAMSON

(*Loudly*)
And if you don't change your tune, you'll get what you're expecting.

MRS WILLIAMSON

It would be better, dear, if you tried to speak less loudly; the workingmen may hear you, you know.

MR WILLIAMSON

(*Shouting louder than ever*)
The working men! What do I care for the working men. Am I depending on them? Did they ever give me anything. Damn them, and you, too.
(*He pushes her roughly from him, so that she knocks over a small fancy table on which are a vase of flowers and some photos.*)

MRS WILLIAMSON

(*Lifting the table & contents*)
If you do not care about the working men, perhaps, you will about the curate, who is in the garden with Clarice, and who is probably charmed with the sound of your sweet voice.

WILLIAMSON

(*Alarmed*)

You wanted him to hear me. You annoyed me purposely, the way he would hear me.

(*The door on left flies open and Clarice runs in.*)

CLARICE

I knew you were fighting with each other again; we could hear your voices from the garden. Will neither of you ever have any sense? Don't you have enough rows without having one when Mr Bishopson is in the house. What sort of people will he think we are. For heaven's sake keep quiet till he goes.

(*Mr Williamson hurriedly replaces the vegetables on the table, and Mrs Williamson starts to sing "Then scatter seeds of kindness" as the curate, following Clarice, enters by door on left.*)

BISHOPSON

Ah! my dear Mr Williamson, how are you.

WILLIAMSON

Well, my dear Bishopson. Glad to see you here. Mrs W and I were just talking about the fine sermon you gave us on Sunday. We enjoyed it, didn't we dear.

MRS WILLIAMSON

Oh, immensely. You spoke straight to the hearts of the poor people, Mr Bishopson.

MR BISHOPSON

It's very good of you to say so. I hope I shall always try to edify, but I'm delighted to think you enjoyed it.

MR WILLIAMSON

You spoke exactly as I would speak.

BISHOPSON

Dear me, it's very nice of you to say so.

CLARICE

Mama, did you tell papa about the way one of his workmen insulted Mr Bishopson?

21

MRS WILLIAMSON

I was just going to mention it, dear, when you came in.

MR WILLIAMSON

Mr Bishopson insulted by one of my men? Then it must have been Rocliffe. That fellow is a hopeless cur.

BISHOPSON

Pray, don't distress yourself, Mr Williamson; I don't in the least mind what he said. I forgive him, for, after all, he is only a poor ignorant man.

MR WILLIAMSON

Oh, you don't know him. He [draws] in men in the works in such a way that you hardly dare speak to them. I sent him here to prevent him from persuading the men to refuse to handle goods that come to us under police protection. I'll have to teach him a lesson. I'll let him see that he can't do what he likes in my house.
(*He goes to door on right, and shouts,* Rocliffe!)

JACK
(*Outside*)
Yes.

WILLIAMSON

Come up here a moment.
(*Jack enters, and, closing the door behind him stands looking at Williamson. Bishopson stands a little behind Williamson watching Jack. Mrs Williamson goes over to the vegetables, and hums a hymn. Clarice goes to the window, & pulling the curtain aside looks out onto the street.*)

MR WILLIAMSON

I have heard a nice story about you.

JACK

Well sir.

WILLIAMSON

Well sir, what sir?

JACK
Well, sir?

WILLIAMSON
Well sir, well sir! damn your cheek—oh, pardon me Mr Bishopson.

{ MRS WILLIAMSON   Melville!
{ CLARICE   Papa!

WILLIAMSON
Are you not satisfied with preaching your unholy doctrines to our men, but you must try to preach them to my family. Well, why don't you answer, man.

JACK
Mr Bishopson will probably be able to inform you that the Church teaches that it is a work of charity to instruct the ignorant.

MR WILLIAMSON
Well I'm—

{ MRS WILLIAMSON   Melville!
{ CLARICE   Papa!

MR WILLIAMSON
Understand, once for all, Rocliffe, that while you are here you must behave yourself. Listen to what is said to you & do what you are told. Don't think because you are local secretary to your confounded union, that you can do what you like. And let me tell you that I think they won't let you hold that job long, for, in spite of all you have said to them, they are handling the goods that come in under police protection.

CLARICE
(*From window*)
There's a great crowd of men in the street.
(*A great shout heard outside*)
Do you hear them shouting.

JACK
I don't believe our men would betray their comrades on strike.

23

WILLIAMSON
You don't! Well you may, for they are doing it now.

JACK
Well, they won't do it long.

WILLIAMSON
Where are you going, Rocliffe?

JACK
I'm going down to the yard to speak to the men.

WILLIAMSON
You'll stop where you are, sir.

JACK
I'll let you see, Williamson, whether you or I am the men's leader.
(*The door on right at back is flung open and Tom rushes in.*)

TOM
Good Lord! They've smashed the kitchen windows.
(*A shout outside, and a stone crashes through the window at which Clarice is standing. She screams, & runs to Bishopson, who crouches down against the wall. Williamson runs to the table and creeps under it.*)

MRS WILLIAMSON
Good Lord, what's that?

WILLIAMSON
(*From beneath the table*)
They're attacking the house. Put out the light, blast you, and don't stand gaping there.

TOM
My God, if they catch me here, they'll think I'm a scab.
(*Another shout as again a stone crashes through the window.*)

MRS WILLIAMSON
They'll not leave a pane of glass in the house. What does it all mean.

JACK

Don't be alarmed Mrs Williamson. It's only the opening hymn of the workers' Harvest Festival.

Curtain.

Act Two

Scene: The Home of the Rocliffes, a tenement in Curzon St. A room which is poorly furnished. A common deal table stands in the centre of the room. At the left is a tiny fireplace. The window is at back. Under the window is a sofa, on which a number of books are lying. To the right of the sofa is a dresser, but the shelves, instead of holding crockery, are packed with books. To the right of this dresser is a door leading down into the street. A small, single bed is at the extreme right of stage. On the wall over the door at right is a picture of the late Queen Victoria, & over the fireplace is a picture of King Billy crossing the Boyne. A washstand with basin & jug stands near the bed in a corner. A few chairs complete the furnishing of the room. The few necessary articles of delph are in the press beneath the dresser. The basin & jug have been taken from the top of the washstand and placed underneath, to make room on top for a pile of writing paper.

Mrs Rocliffe is discovered at the fireplace on which is a small saucepan, the contents of which she is stirring. The table in centre is laid for tea, & is covered with a newspaper instead of a cloth.

As the curtain ascends, Mrs Rocliffe is humming in a vigorous way, the air, "Haste to the Wedding." She is an old woman of about seventy-six years of age. Although afflicted with the infirmities of age, her movements are surprisingly sharp and active. Her eyes are still shining, & her hair is only beginning to turn grey. She has evidently been in her day a very strong, active woman, & still possesses a wonderful reserve of vital force.

MRS ROCLIFFE
(*With a doleful sigh*)
Ah! no; it's the terrible thing to have a sad heart. But I suppose I have had me day, an' I oughtn't to complain. But it was a cold day, an' a bitter day; oftener cold than warm; oftener hungry than full; oftener tired than at ease; oftener sad than merry. But, sure,

I ought to be thankful that I was able to stick it all, an' I always had me health, an' that was somethin'. I wish to God this strike was over, I'm never easy in me mind, the way Jack does be talkin' about things. He has such a terrible temper, though he was always very gentle with me; an' if he got into any trouble, I suppose they'd take the old-age pension off me; not that it'ud be much loss, though we'd miss it now, with nothing else comin' into the house. I hope he'll be in soon; he knows I want to go to the Harvest Festival tonight, an' he promised he'd be in time to get his dinner & tea so that I could go.

(*She begins to sweep the floor.*)

I don't think it'll be long till Higgins turns Turk on us; it's the long, sour face he had on him this mornin' when I went in for a loaf an' some tea an' sugar, because he knew there was no money comin' into the house, an' maybe, wouldn't be for a long time. An' the winter comin' on us too, as well. It would be better for me to be dead than to be sufferin' like this at the end of me days.

(*She again begins to vigorously hum—"Haste to the Wedding," accompanying the tune, with rapid movements of the sweeping brush*)

There is a knock with the knuckles on door at right, and Mrs Duffy enters.

MRS DUFFY

Lord save us, is it workin' again you are! The Divil himself wouldn't keep you easy. Are you goin' to give the clothes to wash for you, this week?

MRS ROCLIFFE

Not this week, Mrs Duffy. With nothin' comin' in how could I expect to pay you. I'll have to manage myself for a while; besides Jack'll help me to wring anything that's heavy, as he often done before.

MRS DUFFY

Go on 'our that an' get them for me, sure, you'll pay me sometime.

MRS ROCLIFFE

I'll be able to do all right this week; I've only a few little things to wash, an' maybe, the strike 'll be over by this time next week.

MRS DUFFY

Blast them for strikes! It's too hot in their leather they're gettin' an' maybe, they'll get a coolin' that'll do them good. It's nourishment half of them want an' not work. I suppose Jack's away in the middle of it.

MRS ROCLIFFE

Oh, indeed you may be sure of it; he's never anywhere else. I['m] never [out] of dread with him since this strike commenced. He's such a hasty boy & he doesn't care what he says.

MRS DUFFY

Bedad, an' he's what you may call a speaker, too. I was listenin' to him last night an' he standin' on a brake, & if you had heard him. Sure, he knocked the divil out of all the rest of them that had their collars an' ties. He has a power of books, Mrs Rocliffe. I don't know how he manages to read all them.

MRS ROCLIFFE

(*Proudly*)

He's always readin'. He takes after his father, an' he may thank himself for his education, for sorra much he went to school; even the Rector says he's very clever.

MRS DUFFY

Then an' the Rector ought to know. He's very fond of Jack, and it nearly broke his heart when Jack began to stop away from Church. Why doesn't he ever come to Church now, Mrs Rocliffe.

MRS ROCLIFFE

It'ud be hard to tell why. I get tired askin' him to go. He talks about the Gospel of Discontent, and when I say that he should try to be content with his lot, he laughs, and puts his arms around me an says, "You don't understand, mother, you don't understand." I don't know what's come over him. And you'd think it was on purpose that all the great ones in the Parish were always askin' me "Where's John?" "Has he given up comin' to Church."

MRS DUFFY

Ah, let them go to Hell, Mrs Rocliffe; what do you care about any of them, as long as you have your son—sorra much they'd give you, or me, either if we wanted it. Sure, the best o' them are only bits o' micks, anyway. When I'm washin' for the Gourley's it'ud give you the sick to see their goin's on. With their court shoes, their silk stockin's an' their ribbons in their camisoles, an' when their brother died there a while ago, they had to pledge half the house to buy their mournin' dresses. I suppose they'll all be there in their style tonight at the Harvest Festival.

MRS ROCLIFFE

I hope Jack'll come in time to let me go.

MRS DUFFY

Can't you leave his tea for him; can't he easily get it himself.

MRS ROCLIFFE

I want to see him tonight—I don't know why—I feel as if there was somethin' terrible goin' to happen.

MRS DUFFY

You're a little fretful, an' no wonder, but the service tonight'ill buck you up a lot. I had a peep at the Church today, an' Mrs Rocliffe, it's glorious. Big bunches of grapes hangin' out o' every gas mantle, and the place where the Baptism Font is nearly hidden with the biggest spuds an' cabbages an' parsnips I ever seen; an' a loaf—oh, so big as that table there standin', as impudent as you please, right in the cintre of the porch—they must have baked it in a special oven, an' apples an' all kinds of fruit around the pulpit and the readin' desk. The Church is like some o' them place[s] that you'd read about in books. But it'll "grey" me to be sittin' all the time, maybe right under a bunch of grapes, when I daren't pull a bloody one o' them.

MRS ROCLIFFE

The collection tonight as well as next Sunday is for the Schools, isn't it.

MRS DUFFY

Sorra bit o' me knows. All I know is there will be a collection—they never forget that. An' those bits of gents with their collars an' cuffs, the sidesmen, hold the plate under your nose, like highwaymen sayin' "Youre money or your life." Sorra, more than a ha'penny they'll get from me, an' it's enough, too, from a poor widda woman. It's givin' me somethin' they ought to be instead of takin' it from me. Here's somebody comin' up the stairs, now, Mrs Rocliffe.

(*The door on right opens, and Jack enters, evidently agitated and in a hurry.*)

JACK

Good evening Mrs Duffy: I haven't a moment to spare, mother. Things are getting lively. They have called out the troops. Some of our Leaders were arrested today. Many of the strikers have been injured, and hundreds are being arrested. A cargo of scabs come over from England tomorrow; may God help any of them that fall into the clutches of the men—never mind what's in the pot, mother; I've no time to wait—a cup of tea will do well.

MRS ROCLIFFE

You'll be killin' yourself runnin' about like this, an' not takin' time to eat a bit. But, sure, you might as well be talkin' to the wall.

(*She fills out Jack's tea, which he takes rapidly; as he takes his tea, he occasionally writes in a notebook which he places beside him on the table*)

MRS DUFFY

Do you think it'ill soon be over, Jack.

JACK

(*Enthusiastically*)

It's going to be a bitter, venomous struggle. The men are more determined than they ever were to gain recognition of their Union. Not that I, personally, care a damn about that. I am not so eager that the men should take some of the power out of the employers hands as I am that they should take, the men should take the whole power into their own; I am not so eager that the men should gain the right towards a living wage as I am that they should overthrow the wage-system altogether. But the time for that is not yet. The Leaders of Labour are as yet like children that have been born out of due season. Sometimes the rank and file are ahead of the Leaders; sometimes the Leaders are ahead of the rank and file. When the advanced thought of the Leaders is fused with the advanced action of the men—then will come the Revolution. But I am talking foolishly, Mrs Duffy, for wisdom consists not in talking of what I understand myself, but in talking of what everybody else understands as well.

MRS DUFFY

Faith, an' you're talkin' Greek to me, Jack.

JACK

The building trade is out today. It's splendid to see the men, to be with them, to be one in fight for human freedom. This fight will go down in History. At last in Ireland the workers have begun to knit the first strands of the Red Cap, which is the only crown for the head of Graunuaile.

MRS DUFFY

Here's somebody else comin' up the stairs now.
(*They all listen. A knock at the door on right, at which Mrs Rocliffe springs up from where she has been sitting at the fire, and, running across the room, opens the door.*)

MRS ROCLIFFE

Oh, it's the Rector. Come in, sir, come in. Jack is just takin' his tea.
(*The Rector accompanied by Mr Bishopson, enters.*)

THE RECTOR

Don't disturb yourself, my dear John; I can easily speak to you as you are taking your tea. I am introducing our new Curate to the Parishioners, who I believe will be a great help to me in my ministry among you all.
(*The Rector is a man of about fifty-five years of age; his hair and beard are quite white; his face is handsome, and is habitually adorned with a*

kind and gentle smile. His whole manner proclaims him to be a refined and cultured gentleman, obviously earnest in his work as a Pastor.)
This is Mrs Rocliffe, Mr Bishopson, than whom there is no more unselfish soul in the Parish; Mrs Duffy, one of our most regular attendants at Divine Service.

MR BISHOPSON
(Very coldly)
I am glad to know you Mrs Rocliffe, and you, too, Mrs Duffy.

THE RECTOR
And this is John, of whom I have spoken to you; one of my most able and spiritual workers in days gone by, one who was always first in the Church and the last to leave it *(brokenly)* one whom it broke my heart to lose; one whom I loved even as my son born, not after the flesh, but after the spirit.

MR BISHOPSON
(more coldly than before)
I have had the honour of meeting Mr Rocliffe before—when he was working in Mr Williamson's house—before he openly indentified himself with the rabble that are on strike.

THE RECTOR
I, too, have always considered it an honour to know John. How are you, my dear, dear boy?

JACK
I am well, thank you, Mr Jennings, and I am grateful for, and fully appreciate the kind opinion in which you continue to hold me, even now.

THE RECTOR
When you were with us in the Church, John, I knew your sincerity and Truth, and that you were as honest as the Sun, and though you are now indentified with a cause that I cannot commend, I still yearn for you, for I know though you have abandoned the Church, you have not abandoned Truth or Honesty.

MRS DUFFY

I had a peep at the Church this mornin' Mr Jennings, an' it's lookin' lovely.

THE RECTOR

Yes, it does look nice. Mr Bishopson, here, deserves all the praise due to its pretty decoration. And, now, my dear John, as well as coming to introduce you to Mr Bishopson, I have also come to appeal to you personally to come tonight to our Harvest Festival. Won't you come, John?

JACK

Not tonight, sir; I have other work to do tonight.

THE RECTOR

I will be preaching tonight John; you often told me how you [liked] my humble efforts to proclaim the Gospel of my Master.

JACK

Not tonight sir; I am sorry, but I have other work to do tonight.

THE RECTOR

Then on Sunday, John; you will come amongst us once again on Sunday. Oh, how it would gladden my heart to see you in the Church again John; the Church in which you were baptised, and confirmed, and in which you often, oh, so often assisted in the cele-bration of Communion; the Church you once loved, John; the Church you once loved. You will, oh, you will be with us on Sunday.

(*A pause.*)

Give me your promise, John.

JACK

If I gave you my promise, sir, I would go.

THE RECTOR

And you will.

JACK

And I will not go.

THE RECTOR

Why, John?

JACK

Because my soul has burst its bonds of patience with the wrong
that makes the life of the class to which I belong unendurable; the
wrong that dooms us to a life of misery before we are born; because I can no longer consent to sell the days that are for [the] days
to come; because I cannot, will not thank God for misery, disease,
poverty and ignorance; Because I no longer believe that the life of
the few should be a perpetual Te Deum, while the lives of the
many should be a perpetual De Profundis; because I am [too]
strong to ignore the sincerity, the truth, the kindliness of an individual in the darkness of the tyranny, and injustice of the system
that he tolerates; because I believe that the joy of Palms and harps
in the next world will not balance the misery of hunger and tenement slums in this one; because—

MR BISHOPSON

This is a pretty sermon to be listening to.

JACK

(*Ignoring him*)

I refuse to call sweet bitter, and bitter sweet, good evil and evil
good; because I hold in contempt those to whom the knowledge
of the truth is all and the practice of it nothing; because I believe
that this strike is the first beat of Ireland's heart towards the freedom of the toiling masses, and, sink or swim, win or lose, I am
with my comrades, heart and soul, mind and body.

MRS DUFFY

There's seven o'clock, an' I forgettin' all about the Harvest Festival.
It'll take me all me time to get me tea an' get ready in time to get
a good seat. So good night to you Mr Jennings an' Mr Bishopson, an' you, Jack, an' it's hopin' I am the strike'ill soon be settled
one way or t'other. I'll not say good night to you Mrs Rocliffe,
for I suppose you'll be in the Church tonight, & if you can man-

age to scooge in don't forget to come up to where I'll be sittin'. (*She goes out, curtseying to the two clergymen.*)

THE RECTOR

Oh, John, you wrong us, you wrong us. You know we sympathise with the poor, with God's own poor. But we cannot escape from the existence of poverty. "The poor we shall always have with us"—the Master says so, and we must, we must believe it. It is our duty to preach patience and submission to God's will to those that sit in the darkness of poverty, for we are told that these light afflictions will work an exceeding weight of glory. And you know, John, that the arms of the Church are ever around the poor; praying with and for them always, advising them constantly, and helping them whenever we can. No other power knows better, or feels more deeply than the Church the terrible conditions under which the very poor live. No matter what you may say, John, I still am convinced that no power loves the poor as the Church loves them; no power does so much to help them on their toiling way through life. But our ways are not your ways, John—

BISHOPSON

God forbid they were.

THE RECTOR

(*Continuing*)

We believe that the real obstacle to social life is selfishness or sin; Violence can accomplish nothing. Evil and good depend upon the heart of man; we can only bring Heaven nearer to ourselves by the elimination of selfishness in its various forms of lust, pride, greed and ambition, and this can only be done by the regeneration and sanctification of the human soul, and there is no power under heaven given among men by which this can be accomplished outside of the Christian Church.

BISHOPSON

You're only wasting your time, sir, talking to him. As knowledge convinces us so ignorance convinces him.

35

THE RECTOR

No time spent speaking on behalf of our Master can ever be wasted, Mr Bishopson, and allow me to remind you that [John] knows more about many things, many important things, than either you or I.

JACK

The time, sir, has gone by for patience. The workers at last are beginning to pull the garlands from the statues of the goddess of Resignation. I know the Church always has her arm around the workers—it is the most effective way to keep them quiet—

BISHOPSON

This is certainly a nice way of talking.

JACK

(*Continuing*)

Oh how you long, how you strive to keep us quiet.

"setting to hymns in Resignation's tone
The slaves' rebellious shout, and wild-ey'd hunger's moan;
For well you know that meek-soul'd patience brews
The drink of comfort made of fees and dues."

You have taught us to remember others and forget ourselves was the only happiness: We have discovered to remember ourselves and forget others is our only security. With me, sir, and with those who have become class-conscious, it is no longer a question of how to alleviate poverty, but a fight to abolish it altogether. You say, sir, violence can accomplish nothing; it has been proved that violence can accomplish anything. It was by violence that the master class secured all that they possess, it is only by violence that they can hold it. Why are the police and the soldiers in the streets today? Why are the scabs armed with revolvers? Simply because the master-class recognises that what you proclaim is weakness to us is the assurance of strength to them. Oh, sir, when we poor workers throng the streets in clamorous efforts to snatch even at the fringe of the good and joyous things of life, it is not the Cross that is held before our faces, but the machine-gun. Is it any wonder then that we grow suspicious and sceptical when the plenty-loving class send the peace loving theologian amongst us to curb our spirits.

BISHOPSON

You are evidently one of those frantic fellows who are anxious to extinguish us theologians.

JACK

No sir; we realize that it is easier to extinguish theologians than it is to prevent the theologians from extinguishing you. But, pardon me, sir, I must be off; I have delayed too long already. Even now I am due at a meeting of the men. Good night, sir, and thank you, thank you, for your kind words and your sincere friendship for one who is unworthy of the friendship of such a man as you.

THE RECTOR

You are not unworthy my dear, dear John; and you will come up to see me some evening, when you are no[t] so busy, come up to tea and we will talk things over in a quiet, friendly way. Won't you promise that?

JACK

Thanks sir, you are very good; perhaps, I shall.

THE RECTOR

You will John, say you will.

JACK

I will, sir with pleasure. I shall never forget your kindness. And, mother, should I be late, don't bother to wait up for me.

MRS ROCLIFFE

Don't go out, tonight, Jack; don't leave me by myself tonight—I feel so lonely, so lonely. And I have such a strange feeling in my heart. Stop with me tonight an' I won't go to the Harvest Festival, but we'll sit together by the fire and talk. It's a long time now since you stayed in with me, and I've no one left now but you, Jack. Stop with me tonight son, only tonight.

JACK

What has you so fanciful tonight, mother? There now, I'll be back as early as I can, and I know you would like to go to the Harvest Festival. Have no fears for me, I am very well able to take care of myself. I am wanted tonight and I know you would not wish me to refuse to share the burden of the men that are fighting for me and for you. I must hurry off—they will be waiting for me. Get yourself dressed and go to Church, and, maybe, I'll be back as soon as yourself. Good night Mr Jennings, good night sir.

THE RECTOR
I am sorry you will not be with us tonight, John; very sorry indeed, but you will remember your promise to come to see me.

JACK
Thank you, I will not forget.
(*He goes out by door on right, and Mrs Rocliffe sits down by the fire in a depressed manner.*)

THE RECTOR
Be of good cheer, Mrs Rocliffe; John is certain to take care of himself for your sake.

MR BISHOPSON
All these labour agitators are particularly aware that self-preservation is the first law of nature.

THE RECTOR
If you knew John as I know him, you would think more of him and less of yourself.

MR BISHOPSON
Pardon me, sir, if I decline to think highly of those who associate themselves with people that glory in the overthrow of all order and all law. I think that it is the duty of a Pastor to admonish them, to warn them, and to plainly show them that they walk in the way of error and not in the way of Truth.

MRS ROCLIFFE
There's no use of warnin' Jack, sir; he's very headstrong, and he'll hold his own opinions against all men. I've often warned him my-

self, but, though, he listens all right, he'll say—"You don't understand, mother, you don't understand." An', maybe, I don't for it's
little schoolin' I got in my young days. An' it's wonderful all the
knowledge he has, an' all the things he's able to talk about. An'
he's a kind an' good son, Mr Jennings. When I'm not well he won't
let me do a hand's turn about the house, an' gives me me break-
fast in bed, an' it's few sons'ud do them things for their mother.

THE RECTOR

He is everything you say, Mrs Rocliffe, a good son, and an excep-
tionally brilliant fellow in every way; he has a warm and a true
heart, and it grieves me deeply to think that he has separated himself from the Church.

MRS ROCLIFFE

An' he was such a regular churchgoer. How happy I used to be
sittin' beside him in the pew, an' he gettin' out the hymns for me,
for me sight isn't as good as it used to be— An', now, I always
have to go by meself, but it's the readin' that has ruined him, the
readin', the readin'; after a while when he began readin' I noticed
a change in him; how quiet he would sit by the fire, thinkin',
thinkin' thinkin', an' I liltin' a song to meself, an' pretendin' not to
watch him. Whenever I spoke to him he wouldn't hear me, or say
yes when he should say no, an' say no when he should say yes.
Whatever he saw in the books I don't know, but they were never
out of his hands. An' from bein' gay an' always laughin' he got
quiet and thoughtful, and for hours an' hours you'd hardly know
he was in the house at all, he was that still an' silent. It was the
readin' that ruined him—the readin', the readin'.

THE RECTOR

Don't be downcast, Mrs Rocliffe; when he comes to see me, we'll
have a long heart to heart talk, and I'm quite confident that it
won't be long till he is back again in his old place in the Church
by the side of his mother.

MRS ROCLIFFE

God grant it, sir.

(*A pause.*
A distant commotion is heard followed by loud shouts.)

MRS ROCLIFFE
My God! What's that happenin' now?

BISHOPSON
Some of John's strikers vindicating law and order, I suppose.

THE RECTOR
Don't be alarmed Mrs Rocliffe; sit down, sit down my dear woman.

MRS ROCLIFFE
For the last few months there's been nothing but rows about here, an' baton charges, an' they have me in such a worry, that the least little thing puts the very heart across me.
(*The disturbance grows louder, followed by several shots.*)

MRS ROCLIFFE
Oh, there's shots, there's shots!

BISHOPSON
The troops must be firing on the strikers; at last they are teaching the scoundrels a lesson.

THE RECTOR
Pray compose yourself, Mrs Rocliffe; be calm; sit down now like a good woman.

MRS ROCLIFFE
Oh, I can't, I can't; oh, if Jack's there—what would I do if anything happen'd to Jack.

THE RECTOR
Nothing will happen to him, Mrs Rocliffe; he is a good boy, and he is in God's hands.

MRS ROCLIFFE
Oh, what would the soldiers care about that; oh Jack, Jack, Jack.
(*Mrs Duffy, fully dressed for the Harvest Festival, rushes in.*)

MRS DUFFY

There's terrible happenin's goin' on down near the Church; you
can't get within sight of it. A crowd is attackin' lorries loaded with
flour or something, an' they're scatterin' the stuff about the streets,
an' murderin' the scabs. An' I saw poor Mr Waugh, the sexton,
an' he tryin' to shut the gate to keep the scabs out, an' his lovely
gown nearly flittered off his back.

MRS ROCLIFFE

Did you see Jack any where, Mrs Duffy.

MRS DUFFY

No, I didn't see Jack; but you couldn't see who was there with
the crowd.

THE RECTOR

Are there no police there.

MRS DUFFY

There was some, but the crowd seemed to be too many for them.

THE RECTOR

Who was it fired the shots?

MRS DUFFY

I don't know, I only heard them.

MRS ROCLIFFE

Oh! Mr Jennings go out an' see if you can see Jack any where;
oh, I'll have no peace till he comes back.
(*The noise grows louder, and dies off.*)

THE RECTOR

There, it's all over now.
(*The sound of voices is heard below, and feet are heard heavily mounting
the stairs.*)

A VOICE

Take him easy, Bill; don't crush him so much, man.
(*The Rector goes out by door, and returns followed by Bill Conway and*

another man carrying Jack in a collapsed condition. Voices [are] heard below, talking in subdued but animated tones.)

BILL

Here Jim, on the sofa; gently, now, boy gently.
(*They stretch Jack down upon the sofa.*)

MRS ROCLIFFE

Oh, my God, my God.

THE RECTOR

In the Name of God, what has happened to John.

BILL

We were attackin' the scabs, sir, an' one o' them shot him.

RECTOR

Has anyone gone for a doctor, quick, has anyone gone for a doctor?

BILL

Three or four of us went off runnin' for a doctor, an' more has gone for the ambulance, though God knows when that'll come for they're havin' a busy time these days.

THE RECTOR

Allow me, dear Mrs Rocliffe; the best thing to do is to keep him perfectly quiet till the doctor comes.

MRS ROCLIFFE

Oh, what'll I do, what'll I do: oh, Jack, Jack, Jack.

JACK

Mother, mother, oh, mother.

MRS ROCLIFFE

My son, my son: ah, Jack, what's happened to you?

JACK

One of the scabs, mother, one of Sir Jocelin Vane's—the Synodsman—scabs shot me, shot me twice.

THE RECTOR

Where are you wounded, John; is it serious, let me open your shirt to look at it.

JACK

They've done for me, sir; I've got it right through the lungs.

MRS ROCLIFFE

Ah, don't say that, Jack; maybe, it's not much, an' the doctor'ill soon be here now.

THE RECTOR

My poor, poor woman, my poor, poor son.

JACK

Lift me up a little, this pain is terrible—Oh God!

MRS ROCLIFFE

For God's sake will no one go for the doctor. Do something for God's sake, Mr Jennings.

JACK

Never mind, mother, never mind the doctor; he'll be here presently, and then I'll be all right. Put your arm around me.

MRS ROCLIFFE

My darling boy, it's terrible to see you this way, an' after all you done for everybody else. Oh, what were they doing when they let the scab shoot you.

BILL

We avenged him well, Mrs Rocliffe; we hit and battered the scab to a pulp an' then threw him into the river.

BISHOPSON

That's, certainly, a nice action to rejoice over.

JACK

It is inevitable sir; we cannot help it even if we would. They are sent out to destroy us, and it would be surprising if we did not sometimes destroy them. It is only one of the terrible tragedies of

43

the economic war. I have been killed by one of my own class, and he has been killed by many of his own class. He because he was not class-conscious, I because I was. But I do not grudge my poor life for the sake of the workers; they have always been welcome to all that I could give them; they are welcome now to the little that remains.

MRS ROCLIFFE

Ah, don't talk like that, Jack; you will break my heart.

JACK

My own dear mother; many a sorrow have I brought upon you.

MRS ROCLIFFE

No, no, Jack. No sorrow, only joy, only joy. Wasn't I always proud of you, an' you such a scholar, an' everybody lovin' you.

JACK

And now I have brought upon you the greatest sorrow of all. But I loved you always, always, mother; loved you and all men.

THE RECTOR

Try not to talk so much, my dear John; you are using up your energy.

JACK

As I always did; as we all always should. Oh! I am getting very, very weak. A drink, oh, give me a drink of water.
(*Mrs Duffy fetches a glass of water to Jack.*)

BILL

I'll run out an' get a sup o' whiskey, Jack; what good is water.

JACK

It's all right, old comrade, never mind; keep your spare money for someone who needs it worse. And, look here, Bill, don't depend too much upon the whiskey.

BILL

No Jack, I'll not; what the Hell is keepin' that bloody ambulance.

44

JACK

Where are you, Bill; I can hardly see you. Here, put your hand on mine, you jailbird. How often were you in jail, Bill?

BILL

Often enough, too often I'm afraid.

JACK

And were you ever really sober Bill?

BILL

Aw, here now, Jack; aw, damit, I was often sober.

JACK

A jailbird and a drunkard—that's what they'd call you Bill; but you have one good feature that outshines all your dark faults—you were always true to your own class.

BILL

(*Brokenly*)

Always, Jack, always. An' always will be, world without end, amen.

JACK

I'm sure of it. I'm proud to spend my last few moments beside you, Bill. Will you give me your hand sir—(*to the Rector*)

THE RECTOR

With all my heart, my dear, dear boy, my son, born not after the flesh but after the spirit.

JACK

(*To Bill*)

You'll take care of my poor old mother, Bill?

BILL

I will, I will; an' I'll give over the drink.

JACK

(*To the Rector*)

You, sir; will you be kind to her who is to spend her last few days in loneliness and sorrow.

THE RECTOR
I will guard her and cherish her for her own sake and for yours.

MRS ROCLIFFE
I don't want anyone, Jack, only yourself, only yourself. Don't talk like that, my son; don't leave me alone in my old age and in my grey hairs.

JACK
Why don't you light the lamp, mother, it's getting very dark.

THE RECTOR
My son, say God have mercy upon me.

JACK
(*Faintly*)
Oh God, may it please thee to succour help and comfort all that are in danger, necessity and tribulation; that it may please thee to preserve all sick persons, all women labouring of child; all young children, and to show thy pity upon all prisoners and captives; that it may please thee to defend and provide for, the fatherless children, and widows, and all that are desolate and oppressed. That it may please thee to have mercy upon all men. That it may—please— thee—to—mother, mother, where are you.

MRS ROCLIFFE
Here my son, here beside you with my arms around you.

JACK
You seem to be far—away—far, far—far away.
(*He falls back dead.*)

THE RECTOR
You may release him, now Mrs Rocliffe; he is gone from us for-ever.
(*The Church Bell rings.*)

MRS ROCLIFFE
Ah, Jack, Jack, Jack, my son, my lovely noble son.

VOICES BELOW

Here it tis, here's the ambulance at last.

BISHOPSON

Come, sir we better be going, there's the bell for the Harvest Festival.

THE RECTOR

I cannot leave this poor woman in this way. Her son could not stop with her tonight and I must take his place.

MRS ROCLIFFE

He's gone from me, my Jack, my Jack, my Jack.

Curtain

Act Three

Scene: Exterior of St. Brendan's. The background consists of a drop curtain depicting a street of ordinary houses in a poor locality. Before this is an iron railing stretching across the stage, which encloses the Church grounds; there is a gate in the centre. On the extreme right of the stage is the west porch of the Church, the door of which is open showing the interior. Heaps of potatoes and all classes of vegetables are visible, as decorations reminiscent of the Festival. A path leads from the porch to the gate at centre back. A few small trees and shrubs ornament the grounds. It is a dark, gloomy night in early November, & the grounds are in gloom, save where the lights in the porch illuminate the immediate vicinity.

Waugh, the sexton, in his gown, comes out of the church; he has a bunch of keys in his hand, and walking along the path to the railings, he opens the gate, and returns to the church porch.

SEXTON

Thanks be to Gawd hit's nearly hall hover. H'I'm tired hof 'andling ton[s] of grapes, putatoes, hand happles, and 'eaps of carrots, honions, turnips and cabbages, without gettin' the chawnce of bringing ha single one hof them 'ome to heat. H'I'm fed hup with them becawse H'I'm not hallowed to be fed hup with them, and I've a good moind to chuck the 'ole job. It's all werk, werk, werk. It's Waugh here an' Waugh there, and Waugh hevery where. A sextant is loike a church weather-cock in a woind a blowing from hevery quarter. He can't turn nowhere, yet he's expected to turn hevery where. And then you must hattend heverything—Prayer-meetin's, Bible Clawsses, Bond o 'ope concerts and chiruch free times hon Sundays. It's 'orrible—human nature couldn't stick it. You have to listen to all sorts of parsons preachin', or the quoir murdering an 'ymn, or some feller ut a Bible Clawss a trying to prove from the Bible that St Peter was never in Rome—as hif hit mattered a 'ang to 'im or me—whether he was or not—and you

48

finking hall the toime of hothers henjoying themselves at the pictures, or having a noice frien'ly chat hover a point hin a pub. And hall for a few bob a week and a 'ouse. Then look at hall the differences of hopinion you have to contend with—Some for the Curate and some for the Rector; some for singin' the hamens and some for saying 'em; 'awf of the congregation accusing the other 'awf of being anti-Cawtholic, and the rest accusing the other 'awf of being anti-Protestant. And the poor sextant is supposed to be able to agree with hall.

Some a 'olding you by the collar and saying, Look 'ere, Waugh, you're an elightened Protestant and you must 'elp us to take these things hout of the church; and hothers catching 'old of your coat and saying—'Ere, Waugh, you're a heddicated churchman and you must 'elp us to bring these things into the Church. They hall 'as me 'awf daft trying to differ and trying to agree. And, now, there's hell about bringing Jack Rocliffe into the church. Anyhow, when the Rector knows the sort he was why can't he let them wake him at home, and not be fighting to bring him here. It won't do him any good and it's bound to do the church hinjury. But 'eadstrong and hall, as the Rector his 'e won't get 'is way this time. Nearly the 'ole parish is against hit. He'll have to yield to the Vestry that are protesting against it. And Sir Jocelyn Vane's in a 'orrible rage about it, for he looks upon it has a personal hinsult. If he hopposes the Rector it's bound to be a wash-out; the Rector daren't go against his best subscriber. As for me, I won't 'ave nothing to do with it.

(*The Rector appears in the porch.*)

THE RECTOR
Waugh.

THE SEXTON
Yessir.

THE RECTOR
Get the trestles and place them in the church in the centre of the chancel.

WAUGH

If I might make bold enough has to say anything—

THE RECTOR

You will just do what you are told, Waugh.

THE SEXTON

Yessir.
(*The Rector goes into the church.*)

THE SEXTON

'E's agoing to spoil the 'ole service, 'e is.
(*The Williamsons enter by the gate and proceed towards the church.*)

WILLIAMSON

I will certainly leave the church if he persists in his folly.

MRS WILLIAMSON

How greatly they would miss your sweet face, dear.

WILLIAMSON

This is neither the time nor the place to be funny, madam.

CLARICE

Oh, for God's sake let the pair of you shut up sometime. If you leave, papa, Mr Bishopson should resign, too.

MRS WILLIAMSON

What can you expect from a church that thinks more about Baptism than Conversion; from which has been banished the pure gospel offered freely to all, without money and without price.

WILLIAMSON

We can expect, and we must insist upon everything being done, as St Paul says, in decency and order. Imagine the Rector preferring the scoundrel Rocliffe, who even hadn't the decency to acknowledge the church by his presence at the services, and who said and did such terrible things, to me, or, say Sir Jocelyn Vane. It's outrageous, preposterous. I won't have, I won't have it. Sir Jocelyn may tolerate if he likes but I won't—the fellow that laughed, actually laughed when the crowd were smashing every window in our house—it's perfectly maddening.

CLARICE
The sooner we get a new Rector the better. Mr Jennings is getting very old, and old people do queer things.

WILLIAMSON
(*Condescendingly*)
Good night Waugh; have any of the Vestry arrived yet?

SEXTON
Hall of 'em, sir; they're down in the Vestry, now, with Sir Jocelyn Vane.

WILLIAMSON
And where's the Rector?

SEXTON
He's in the Vestry too, sir, I suppose.

MR WILLIAMSON
Slip down and tell Bishopson to come up here for a moment.

SEXTON
Yes, sir. (*He goes into the church.*)

WILLIAMSON
I really dread meeting the Rector; I feel very uncomfortable when he looks at me; he looks at one so strangely.

MRS WILLIAMSON
If you thought more of the pure Evangel and less of his High-Church nonsense, you wouldn't be so much afraid of him.

MR WILLIAMSON
Who's afraid of him; if I—

CLARICE
Oh, hush here's Mr Bishopson.
(*Mr Bishopson comes out of the church.*)

BISHOPSON

Oh, good night Mrs Williamson, good night sir; my dear Miss Williamson come in out of the sharp night air.
(*He shakes hands all round.*)

WILLIAMSON

Well, how are things going on?

BISHOPSON

The Rector is still obstinate; he refuses to obey the Vestry—indeed, he refuses even to hear what they have to say.

WILLIAMSON

But this is most illegal; what's the good of having a Vestry if the Rector can override its decisions. It's simply monstrous.

BISHOPSON

If the Rector persists in his obstinancy, I fear the parish will lose a number of its most liberal subscribers.

WILLIAMSON

Serve him right—that's the only way to deal with these people and bring them to their senses—close your purse.
(*The Rector comes out of the church and stands on the steps of the porch; he is dressed in a cassock, and has a square black velvet cap on his head.*)

THE RECTOR

Good night to you all.
(*There is an awkward silence.*)

Then MRS WILLIAMSON *says*

Come on Clarice, we may as well go in. (*& passes the Rector with Clarice without noticing him.*)

BISHOPSON

(*Suavely*)

Don't you really think, sir, you ought to go down and speak with the members of the Vestry?

THE RECTOR

It would be useless; they all have hardened their hearts.

WILLIAMSON

But don't you realize, sir, that it is very dangerous to run counter to the clearly expressed wishes of the Vestry.

THE RECTOR

My conscience is quite clear on the matter. Would to God we were all as worthy to meet death as poor John Rocliffe. To me all men are alike; I dare not refuse any whom my Master would welcome. Oh, Mr Williamson, have a little pity upon the dead boy's lonely mother.

WILLIAMSON

But my dear sir, we cannot go against the wishes of the Vestry.

THE RECTOR

The wishes of my Master are paramount to the wishes of my Vestrymen; I cannot turn a man away because he may be a Fenian, a Trades' Unionist or an Orangeman; for the Master hath said— "Him that cometh to me I will in no wise cast out."
(*Bill enters by gate and comes down.*)

BILL

Skuse me, mates, which of yous is the Rector.

THE RECTOR

I am he, my good man.

BILL

Well, sir, the men sent me down to see if you was ready to receive the body.

THE RECTOR

Quite ready; let it be brought to the Church immediately; Service will start shortly.

BILL

We're only waitin' for the word sir, though most of the men is bringin' him here against their will, for they'd rather wake him in the Union Hall, where we could all be near our comrade.

THE RECTOR

Your rough love for your comrade does you credit, my good man, but this is a more meet place in which to enfold the body of our dear brother till we commit him to the grave.

BILL

Right you are, sir; I'm sure the boys is agreeable, seein' he was a Protestant.

WILLIAMSON

And what religion are you, my man.

BILL

A poor kind of a Catholic but a damn good Union man.

WILLIAMSON

What do you work at?

BILL

(*Proudly*)

I'm a docker, sir.

BISHOPSON

A docker; what's that?

BILL

One as puts in and takes things out of ships; an' the best stuff in the Labour Movement.

BISHOPSON

You drink, I suppose; you certainly look like a man that does.

BILL

I used to, but I've given it up. I've had ne'er a drink since Jack was kilt; me happy drinkin' days is all over now, for I have to look after poor Jack's poor 'oul mother. You see, sir, I gave him my word I'd do it.

BISHOPSON

(*Sarcastically*)

And of course a man like you would never break his word.

BILL

(*Seriously*)

Never, sir; I might break the head of a policeman or a scab, but me word, never. Jack often tried to make me promise to give up the drink, but I always refused for I knew if I gave me promise I'd keep it.

THE RECTOR

Honesty and Truth clothed in the garments of shame.

BISHOPSON

(*To Williamson*)

Villainy and deceit decked in the gaudy garments of insolence; I'm almost beginning to believe that the Rector is taking leave of his senses, when he can discover anything good in such a low type of humanity as that man is.

WILLIAMSON

It is simply shocking and disgusting in a man of his learning, his experience and his position. The select Vestry will, in the future, have to take everything into their own hands.

BISHOPSON

No other course seems to be open; we cannot possibly allow such actions to continue unchecked—one can never tell where they may lead to—It is a most dangerous thing to encourage these people in their evil ways, and to set them up against responsible and respectable people who have a stake in the country.

THE RECTOR

My dear friend, be good enough to go and tell your comrades to bring the body of our dear departed brother to the church as soon as they can.

BILL

I'm off, sir; everything was almost ready when I left them an' we were only waitin' for the band to come to start.

BISHOPSON

A Band! Surely, you can't mean to bring a band here—and on a Sunday, too.

BILL

What's the harm in a band sir? You don't think anything'ud stop the boys from turnin' out, and showin' their respects to a comrade that has given his life for them?

BISHOPSON

(*To the Rector*)

Surely, sir, you will not tolerate this terrible profanation of the Sabbath day?

RECTOR

I'm afraid we tolerate too many things that are a greater profanation to the Lord's Day, than this simple and rough manifestation of sorrow and of love. We strain at gnats and swallow camels.

BISHOPSON

This is beyond the endurance of a conscientious minister of the Protestant Church.

(*He passes quickly by the Rector into the church.*)

WILLIAMSON

It is perfectly scandalous; what on earth will the Vestry say about this lastest piece of play-acting.

(*He passes quickly by the Rector into the Church.*)

BILL

Is the Band not to come, sir? We'll only be playin' the Dead March, an' no Catholic Hymns or Sinn Fein tunes.

THE RECTOR

Do all you think proper to honour the memory of your poor comrade for God knows, he deserved it all.

BILL

Right sir an' thank you heartily.

(*Bill goes out by gate.*)

THE RECTOR

(*Walking slowly up and down the path*)

Oh, God, how easy it is to be good, how hard it seems to be pitiful. But it is not goodness, it cannot be goodness.

Though where there is pity there may be no goodness, there can be no goodness where there is no pity. My poor boy, my poor boy, they are not content with the life of thy body, but would even strive to lay violent hands on thy soul. Oh, it is brutal, unchristian, savage, to oppose the desire that his poor tired body might repose for a few short hours in the Church that he once loved so well. Their hatred is as cruel as the savage who mutilates the body of his victim. It is a terrible and sinful gratification of the lust of hatred. I will oppose it I must oppose, for my own sake and for theirs. And yet I doubt that I am acting wisely to deliberately turn my flock into a pack of wolves by persisting in an action that they consider to be highly reprehensible. If I do this thing my influence with them is gone for ever, gone forever, gone forever. But I cannot turn back now, I cannot, I cannot. What could I say to his comrades, what could I say to his poor afflicted mother. What would they think of me! They would regard me with contempt and the contempt would be richly deserved. And yet they might have more pity upon me than those to whom I looked for encouragement and support. This terrible, terrible unrest of the lower-classes is overthrowing all our long-settled ideas of peace and happiness. It has shaken my poor little parish to its very foundations, and today we are a house sharply divided against itself. What will the end of it all be what will the end if it all be? When shall we love one another as we ought to do? Oh, we are firm in the Faith, steadfast in Hope, but we have abandoned Charity, and the greatest of these is Charity.

(*Mrs Rocliffe enters by gate, accompanied by Mrs Duffy. Sir Jocelyn Vane, Bishopson and Williamson come out from the church.*)

WILLIAMSON

The Vestry urgently request you to come down and speak to them before anything is definitely done, sir.

THE RECTOR

It would be useless for me to go down to them, Mr Williamson; they would refuse to listen to me.

SIR JOCELYN

(*He is a short, very stout, stumpy little man, with the stamp of the wealthy dominant merchant, sure of himself, and confident that all others less wealthy than him self will bow to his assurance—upon him. His apologetic prefaces serve only to emphasise his settled belief that nobody could possibly oppose whatever he may say, or whatever he may wish. He has a large round head, brilliantly bald, & he has a habit of drawing his hand over it; as if he expected that some moment his hair will grow again in deference to his wishes, and seems surprised at the delay.*)
Pardon me, Mr Jennings, for suggesting that what you probably meant to say was that you would refuse to listen to the Vestry.

THE RECTOR

I'm afraid that is an unjust remark, Sir Jocelyn; I always have had the liveliest [respect] for the opinions and advice of my Vestry, but to yield to them in the circumstances of the present dispute would mean the utter abandonment of my sacred prerogatives as a pastor of souls. Their decision is not a just decision, it is not a merciful decision, for prejudice, hard and pitiless, has entrenched itself in their hearts.

SIR JOCELYN

Pooh, pooh, sir: Pardon me for saying that it is anything but prejudice; the Vestry is solely animated by sentiments of dignity due to themselves, to the Church—and to me, sir; for you will kindly remember that it was my driver that shot Rocliffe in self-defence for which he was brutally murdered, and notwithstanding all this, sir, you actually wish to force us to identify ourselves with a rabble whose self-expression is manifested in violence and murder, by allowing the obsequies, or part of them, at least, of this dead agitator to be held in this church. Surely, you cannot expect me to associate myself with such an action.

THE RECTOR

I expect you to have mercy, as you shall hope for mercy yourself some day, Sir Jocelyn.

SIR JOCELYN

Mercy! What mercy had he or his comrades on my driver who was simply doing his duty to God and Society.

THE RECTOR

We can do nothing now but pray that God may have mercy on their souls. In the case of our poor dead brother—

SIR JOCELYN

Pardon me, he was no brother of mine.

WILLIAMSON

nor of mine.

THE RECTOR

(*Continuing*)

Judgement has been taken out of our hands, and to deny his body the last tribute that the Church—of which he was a member—can give would be a perilous act of presumption.

SIR JOCELYN

You forget, sir, his whole life was a perilous presumption, perilous to the Church and perilous to Society, till at last, thank God, it became perilous to himself.

THE RECTOR

Every Sunday we pray that God may have pity upon all men, are we to refuse to have pity upon some?

SIR JOCELYN

I refuse to argue the matter further; but, allow me to assure you, sir, that if you are determined to identify yourself, and through yourself, to identify the Church, with those who have committed themselves to the overthrow of established Society, and with Society, to overthrow the Church—for we all know that the safety of the Church depends upon the stability of Society—then, sir, you will not have Sir Jocelyn Vane with you; and I humbly beg to say that the contingency of the withdrawal of my support is a subject worthy of a little consideration.

BISHOPSON
A most serious consideration, indeed.

WILLIAMSON
It would be nothing short of a calamity for our church to lose your support, Sir Jocelyn; nothing short of a calamity, and all for a silly and sentimental attachment to an individual whom we all know was a scoundrel.

THE RECTOR
Mr Williamson, Mr Williamson, for shame! De mortuis nil nisi bonum.

WILLIAMSON
Oh, we don't want to be listening to any of your popish Latin.
(*Mrs Williamson and Clarice come out from the church.*)

MRS WILLIAMSON
Waugh has actually placed trestles in the chancel, and when we ventured to object he told us he did so by the Rector's orders. We certainly will not remain in the church while those things are there. Be good enough, Melville, to take me and Clarice home.

CLARICE
And you had better go in, Papa, and take away your carpet and cushions out of our pew.

MRS ROCLIFFE
An' why did you promise to bring my poor Jack into the Church, if you didn't want to do it?

SIR JOCELYN
We never promised such a thing, my good woman.

MRS ROCLIFFE
Oh, yes you did; the Rector made me make all arrangements.

SIR JOCELYN

The Rector acted without the knowledge and against the wishes of the Select Vestry.

MRS ROCLIFFE

But you will let him in—you won't shame me before everybody at the last moment.

THE RECTOR

Have pity, Sir Jocelyn, on this poor heartbroken mother.

SIR JOCELYN

There is a time for everything, sir; this is the time for perfectly just, if, unhappily, stern measures. You can choose between her and me.

WILLIAMSON

I thoroughly agree with Sir Jocelyn; pity here would be a condonement of crime and disorder.

MRS ROCLIFFE

And this is the kind of Christians you are; now I see it was no wonder my Jack's hand was raised again' you.

SIR JOCELYN

There! You see, sir, it is perfectly useless to have pity upon these people.

WILLIAMSON

It only makes them worse.

MRS DUFFY

Shh, Mrs Rocliffe, don't you know that's Sir Jocelyn Vane that's talkin'.

MRS ROCLIFFE

An' what's Sir Jocelyn Vane to me? Wouldn't I give a thousand Sir Jocelyn Vanes to get back my dear Jack.

SIR JOCELYN

It's plain to be seen that the mother is as bad as the son. He evidently taught her well.

MRS ROCLIFFE

He taught me nothing, but he loved me well. But I have eyes to see an' ears to hear, an' a heart to feel, an' I can understand now that there was wisdom in his foolishness. I wouldn't let him into your church, now; no, not if you all went down on your bended knees to me. Those that love him'ill bury him an' we'll owe no thanks to you, for only for the likes of you I'd have my own lovely son beside me today. Ah, Jack, Jack, Jack.

THE RECTOR

Pray, Mrs Rocliffe, try to be calm.

MRS ROCLIFFE

Be calm; how can I be calm an' they callin' my dead son a scoundrel an' every thing that is sinful: my boy that loved every thing an' every body.

(*Bill comes quickly through the gate to the church.*)

BILL

The boy's are comin' along now, he'll be here in a few minutes.

MRS ROCLIFFE

Bring him back, Bill. He's not goin' into the church; they won't let him go in. He's not good enough for them—
He was a scoundrel, an' even in death, he's not good enough to be beside respectable Christians.

BILL

Not to be brought into the church, why?

SIR JOCELYN

We scarcely think it necessary to explain the reason to you, my man; and even were we foolish enough to do so, you would probably not have the intelligence to understand.

BILL

Maybe you're right, and I wouldn't be able to understand you, but the day'll come when we will compel you to understand us.

WILLIAMSON

Now, then, sir, none of your labour talk here; this is not your

Trades' Union Rooms; you have no right to be here at all, so you had better go back to your comrades.

BILL

Would you shift me?

BISHOPSON

(*To Mrs Williamson and Clarice*)
Come my dear Mrs Williamson, & Miss Clarice, this is not the conversation for your delicate ears; allow me to bring you into the church.

CLARICE

Things have certainly come to a nice pass when a low labourer can insult my papa beside the church in which he is the chief member of the congregation.
(*Bishopson, Clarice & Mrs Williamson go into the church. Mrs Duffy slips in after them.*)

WILLIAMSON

Now, sir, none of your violent talk; (*to the Rector*) Will you tell him to leave us, sir.

THE RECTOR

I often thought that a priest-ridden laity was a terrible tyranny, but a laity-ridden priesthood is a more terrible one. (*To Bill*) I am so sorry, my good man; but you see what we contemplated is impossible; my parishioners won't allow it. May God have mercy upon me and forgive them.

MRS ROCLIFFE

You are just as bad as the rest of them; you are afraid to go again' them; you got me to agree to bring my poor boy to the church an' now you're goin' back on your word. My poor, poor Jack was right—the Church is always again' the workin'-class.
(*The Dead March is heard in the distance.*)

WILLIAMSON

(*Excitedly*)
Here they're comin', for God's sake get them away before the

crowd gets here—this sort of people would think nothing of attacking the Church, and, may be, kill some of us.

BILL

So you're afraid of the throngs of the workers, Mr Minister's man are you? But, by God, one o' these days when we get goin' you and your friends, the Sir Jocelyns, 'ill have good cause for tremblin' in their shoes.
(*Sir Jocelyn, choking with anger is about to retort, when Williamson pulls him violently into the church.*)

WILLIAMSON

For God's sake, Sir Jocelyn, say nothing to provoke that blaguard; he might excite the crowd, & you cannot tell what they would do if they were aroused, and half of them, maybe, drunk.

BILL
(*As they are entering the church*)
Go on Sir Jocelyn, and sing your psalms an' read your Bible, an' thump your craw, an' ask God to have mercy on you for you'll need it one of these days. We'll stan' by the man that kep' himself down by fightin' the rich, again' them that lifted themselves up by fighting the poor.
(*The Sexton and Mr Bishopson come down from the Church.*)

SEXTON

Mr Bishopson says, sir, I'm to take the trestles where the coffin was to go, away.

THE RECTOR
(*Slowly*)
Yes, Waugh, you may take them away again.

MRS ROCLIFFE

An' I may take me poor boy away, as well. Oh, God be praised he was never beholdin' to any of you. Come on, Bill, I have one poor friend, thank God.

64

BILL

Ay, till death do us part, so help me God!

WAUGH
(*On church steps*)
It wants only twenty minutes to the hour, sir. Shall I ring the bell?

THE RECTOR
(*Slowly*)
Yes, you may start to ring now.
(*The Bell rings.*)

MRS ROCLIFFE
(*Going up path towards gate*)
Oh, my son, my lovely boy. My son, my Jack. You are gone from your poor old mother, forever—ah Jack, Jack, Jack, my son, my son.

BILL

Don't fret, Mrs Rocliffe; we avenged him well: didn't we beat an' batter the scab that shot him, and then flung what was left of him into the river. Doesn't that cheer you up a bit?

MRS ROCLIFFE
I don't know, Bill, I don't know; maybe he, too, was the only son of some poor, old, heartbroken mother.
(*The crowd outside the church grounds are heard singing.*)
   The people's flag is deepest red,
    It shrouded oft our martyred dead;
   And ere their limbs grew stiff and cold,
    Their hearts' blood dyed its every fold.
  Then raise the scarlet standard high,
    Beneath its shade we'll live and die;
   Tho' cowards flinch and traitors sneer,
    We'll keep the red flag flying here.
(*Bishopson in his surplice comes from church.*)

BISHOPSON
You had better come, sir, and get ready for the Harvest Festival.

THE RECTOR

The Harvest Festival! O God may it please thee to succour, help and comfort all that are in danger, necessity and tribulation; to defend and provide for, the fatherless children, and widows and all that are desolate and oppressed.

(*The crowd singing outside.*)

> Ah! well it tells of triumphs past
> It speaks the hope of peace at last;
> The standard bright, the symbol plain,
> Of human right and human pain.
> Then raise the scarlet standard high
> Beneath its shade we'll live and die;
> Tho' cowards flinch and tyrants sneer
> We'll keep the Red Flag flying here.

THE RECTOR

Oh, God, that it may please thee to have mercy upon all men.

BISHOPSON

Come on, sir, the people will be coming in a few moments to the Harvest Festival.

The Rector turns to go into the church as the

Curtain Falls.

APPENDIX
Revised Version (incomplete) of Act One

Scene: The parlour or sitting-room of the Williamsons. It is furnished not to ensure the comfort or to demonstrate the refinement of the occupiers, but to affect those who may be visitors with a sense of plenitude in household goods. Every thing is as vivid and as glaring as possible: pictures crowd together on the walls, interspersed with such Scriptural mottoes as, "God is Love"; "Watch and Pray, Lest ye enter into Temptation"; "The Earth is full of the Goodness of the Lord." The doors, one of which is on left side of stage, & the other at back on the Right hand side, are painted in sky blue panels & white borders. The window, ornamented with the same colours, is at back of stage to the left side; between this window and the second door is a piano, over which is a boldly lettered Scriptural motto— "Sing Praises unto the Lord." At one side of the window is a pink delph pedestal surmounted by a green delph flower pot, in which is an artificial plant, on the other side is a green delph pedestal surmounted by a pink flower pot containing another artificial plant. Brightly upholstered chairs stand around the room with an air of impressive dignity, and on the table, covered with a crimson cloth, is a huge family Bible. The fireplace is on the Right, & its furnishings are of shining brass.

The floor is garnished with a gaudy carpet, and a white hair rug is stretched before the fire place.

At present newspapers cover the furniture nearest the fireplace, and the white rug has been removed and laid upon the sofa, which is enriched by a few highly coloured cushions.

Tom is discovered [putting in] the last few coloured tiles in the hearth. He is bent down over his work, and is smoking diligently. The door at the Back Right of stage opens and [Jim], who has a sweeping brush in his hand, enters, and looks curiously around.

TOM
(*Who has violently snatched the pipe out of his mouth, & on seeing who has entered, replacing it again between his lips*)

67

Why the hell don't you whistle when you're comin' in; I thought it was that old rip comin' back again.

[JIM]
Wasn't she here when I went down for the brush; how could I tell she was gone. What singular inducement tempted her to leave your sweet society?

TOM
There was a knock at the door, and she galloped out of the room; I suppose she went to see who was knockin'. I'll not be sorry when I get out of this place; my head is going wild with the hymns she's always singin'.

[JIM]
(*Goes over and opens the family Bible; he takes up a pen and heavily marks some passage, replaces the pen, and leaves the Bible open on the table.*)
Ever since we came here to do this job she's been watchin' and pimpin', afraid to leave [me] in the room for a bloody minute.

[JIM]
She distrusts you, Tom. She [is] evidently afraid you'd steal the Bible.

TOM
She'll wait a long time before I'd be bothered with her Bible.

[JIM]
She doesn't know you so well as you know yourself, Tom. What do you care about Bibles or Prayerbooks?

TOM
(*indignantly*)
I said nothing again' Prayer-books—that is certain kinds of prayer-books.

[JIM]
Ay, the ones with the trade-mark of your own particular creed

upon them. Prayer, Tom is only a faint ruby fairy light in this world which is Hell.

TOM

I won't listen to that kind of talk—give us that straight edge.

[JIM]
(*as he hands over the straight edge*)
Do you know Swinburne, Tom.

TOM
(*meditatively*)
Swinburne—Swinburne—is he a brick[ie] or a labourer?

[JIM]
Neither you poor unenlightened soul. He's a poet.

TOM
What the hell do I want to know about poets!

[JIM]
Just about as much as you want to know about Bibles, I suppose. This is what Swinburne says about prayer:—

> "The ghosts of words and duty dreams,
> Old memories, faiths infirm and dead,
> Ye fools; for which among you deems
>   His prayer can alter green to red,
>   Or stones to bread?"

TOM
I'm not goin' to listen to that kind of talk. Come on down till we cut this other tile—I'm not sorry it's the last—I wish we had the kitchen range done now so that we could say goodbye to her and her hymns. *Exit by door on left, [Jim] following.*
(*Melville Williamson enters by door on the right at back. Williamson is a man of about fifty-five years of age—he [is] beginning to become corpulent, due probably to the need of exercise. He walks over to the fireplace & looks at the work that Tom and [Jim] have been doing.*)

WILLIAMSON

My God! They haven't that little bit of a job done yet. I'll have to get rid of that Driscoll, he's getting too damn impudent altogether. Even threats of dismissal has no effect on him. They're a ripe lot, the whole of them—workmen, wife and [blank] (*He crosses over to the table, and sees the Bible open:*) Up to her tricks again, eh, my lady. You think you'll vex me with your Bible markin', but you never made a bigger mistake in your life. (*he reads the marked passage:*) "And though I bestow all my goods to feed the poor, and though I give my body to be burned, and have not charity, it profiteth me nothing.

"Charity suffereth long and is kind; charity envieth not; charity vaun[t]eth not itself, is not puffed up.

"Doth not behave itself unseemly, seeketh not her own, is not easily provoked, thinketh no evil."

Oh! what a glorious thing it is to have a saintly wife! that is not easily provoked and thinketh no evil! a wife so good that in the effort to make a heaven of everybody's home she makes a hell of her own. She's been meddling with my books again. Damn her, can she leave nothing alone!

(*He crosses to door at back of stage on the right, opens it and shouts—*) Eh, are you there! do you hear, where did you put my book with the list of subscriptions to the Susentation Fund. Are you there. Will you come up here when you hear yourself called. Damn it are you deaf.

(*Mrs Williamson enters, humming a hymn.*)

MRS WILLIAMSON

Well, dear husband, do you want me.

MR WILLIAMSON

Want you! God forbid I ever wanted the like of you—I'd be in a bad way.

MRS WILLIAMSON

I thought I heard your sweet voice calling me, dear.

MR WILLIAMSON
If you left things where I left them, you—

MR WILLIAMSON
Where did you put that book with the names of the subscribers?

MRS WILLIAMSON
Don't you think my dear if you open'd your eyes, & looked for it you would be able to find it.

MR WILLIAMSON
Tell me where you put the book, and give over your damned sarcastic prate.

MRS WILLIAMSON
I'm not inclined to dance attention on you; look for it my dear husband; seek and ye shall find.

MR WILLIAMSON
(*Walking angrily over to her and grasping her arm*)
Tell me where the book is before I lose my temper; do you want me to knock you down?

MRS WILLIAMSON
Whether I want you or not: I am sure you would like to. Indeed, ever since I had the joy to become your dear wife, I am expecting that exhibition of love, my dear.

MR WILLIAMSON
And, I tell you, you jade, unless you change your manners, you'll get what you're expectin'.

MRS WILLIAMSON
Don't you think my dear, you ought to try and speak less loudly; the workingmen may hear you, you know.

MR WILLIAMSON
(*Shouting, more loudly than ever*)
What do I care about the workingmen! Am I depending on them! do they give me anything! Blast them and you, too!—

He pushes her firmly from him, so that she knocks down a little table on which are a vase of flowers and some photos that fall with a crash, and goes out by door on [blank] shutting it violently behind him, as Tom and [Jim] re-enter by door on [blank].

MRS WILLIAMSON

(Picks up table and rearranges the fallen articles; as she is doing this she sings the hymn:)

Let us gather up the sunbeams, lying all around our path;
Let us keep the wheat and roses casting out the thorns and chaff.
Let us find our sweetest comforts in the blessings of today
With a patient hand removing all the briers from the way!
Then scatter seeds of kindness, then scatter seeds of kindness
Then scatter seeds of kindness for our reaping by and by!

TOM

(Putting in the last tile)

She's at it again. It's a wonder she has the cheek to be singin' hymns after what has happened. They're a happy pair of doves, aren't they, Jim.

JIM

(To Mrs W.)

That's a nice song you're singin' ma'am.

MRS WILLIAMSON

That's a hymn, my good man, and not a song. I never sing songs, they are of the earth, earthy: I try always to think of higher things. The profane world is nothing to me. What will happen to me hereafter is more to me [than] what happens now. I am Eternity's heir, not the creature of Time.

JIM

An' I hope you won't be disappointed ma'am. It would be a great shock after denying ourselves by praying, & singing hymns and making ourselves miserable all our lives for things after this life not to be what we expect.

72

MRS WILLIAMSON

Your faith is feeble poor man. There is no fear in the hearts of those who know they are saved. But I can see you are but a poor perishing soul. To be in doubt is to be lost. Oh! You must not know your Bible: do you read your Bible every day?

JIM

I'm sorry to say I don't, ma'am. You see I'm not able to read; I can only write a little.

MRS WILLIAMSON

How dreadful not to be able to read the Bible! I suppose you'r not a Protestant.

JIM

I'm supposed to be one, ma'am. I used to go to Church, now an' again; but I haven't gone now for years: bad company led me astray.

TOM

Give us another little bit o' grout, Jim, an' don't be talkin' through your hat. You'll have her on to the pair of us in a minute.

MRS WILLIAMSON

Give them up! Come away from them lest they lure your soul to destruction. Pray, & you will be delivered out of their hands.

JIM

I'm afraid prayer would be no use in my case. Swinburne—that's one of my particular butties, ma'am—says that those who pray are fools. He's a bit of a poet, and he made up a song about prayer; one of the verses runs like this:—

> Do the stars answer? in the night
> Have ye found comfort? or by day
> Have ye seen gods? What hope what light
> Falls from the farthest starriest way
> On you that pray?

MRS WILLIAMSON

That's a strange song, & full of sinful vanity. Oh! don't believe what the Devil's children write or sing. They do these things to entice us from the way of truth, which is the way of Salvation. If you had kept to your Bible and your hymns you would never have learned that. That fellow—whoever he is—writes such things, because he loves cursin' an' swearin' an' all manner of iniquity. Keep far from him; he is one who loves sin and will not give it up, for the Lord has hardened his heart.

JIM

My other buttie, Shaw, ma'am, would tell you there was no such thing as sin, and Walt Whitman said to me one day in a pub, when we were drinkin' a pint together, that in himself & in everyman there was much good and evil; and that there was no evil, & if there was it was good and important to himself, to the land and to me. So it's hard for a poor innocent ignorant fellow like me to be able to resist such powerful sayin's.

MRS WILLIAMSON
(Gushingly)
Oh, my poor wandering lamb. I wish you'd come to our Hall in Gospel Street on Monday and Wednesday nights. The services are so bright, and we all do be so happy. And then you could come to church on Sundays, Saint Denis's you know, where Mr W. is Churchwarden and Synodsman—he was elected at the last Vestry meeting, no one but was delighted that he agreed to take the positions—and I would speak to the Rector about you. I'm sure he would be glad to help you—and I have some little books about Eternal Life and eternal Death that I must give you—(she goes over to a cabinet and takes out a little coloured book) and see here is the whole Gospel in coloured leaves.—See the first leaf black, the second red, the third white and the last one gold—meaning of course the blackness of sin, the Blood of Christ; the white one, the state of salvation, and the gold leaf the glory that shall be the gift to every believer.—Come my dear man to our Hall, & we'll try to save you; don't be afraid—remember the promises of the Bible.

JIM

No use, ma'am; those promises are not for such as I.

MRS WILLIAMSON

Yes they are, oh! yes they are! They are for all. (*Sings:*)
"Whosoever will, whosoever will
Send the proclamation over vale and hill;
'Tis the loving Father calls the wanderer home,
Whosoever will may come!"
(*Mr W. enters suddenly by door on [blank]; listens to Mrs W. singing, and then advances:*)

MR WILLIAMSON

I wish to God, Mrs W. that you'd let these fellows attend to their work, and not be giving them an excuse to idle their time. And you shouldn't forget Jim [blank] that you're not far from the gate. It appears that you're not satisfied with making the men discontented but you must even act the fool in your foreman's house.

JIM

I suppose one of the Rights of Man is the priviledge of acting the fool in his own house, and here, doubtlessly the right belongs to you.

MR WILLIAMSON

It won't be long till you get a cooling my fine fellow.

JIM

Better a cooling here than to be too hot hereafter.—so Mrs Williamson says.

MR WILLIAMSON

Mind your work, & never mind Mrs Williamson. You, anyhow, have no right to speak this way. Are you nearly done there?

JOE
Done here now, sir.

MR WILLIAMSON

Well get on down to the kitchen, then, to the other job, and stir yourselves, or it will be the last job you'll idle over here.
(*Joe gathers up his tools & goes out by door on [blank] Jim follows, turning as he reaches the door, and bowing to Mrs W.*)

JIM

Domine Vobiscum.

MRS WILLIAMSON

(*Involuntarily to Mr W.*)
What's that he said?

MR WILLIAMSON

How the hell do I know. It's a wonder you'd let a common labourman cod you up to your face.

MRS WILLIAMSON

Cod me! He did nothing of the sort. He has a soul to save as well as you, even though he is an ignorant labourer.

MR WILLIAMSON

Ignorant! By heavens if you know as much as he does, you might sensibly crow a little louder than you do.

MRS WILLIAMSON

Well, I'm able to read and write, a little at all events.

MR WILLIAMSON

You are certainly able to talk, my dear Jane.

MRS WILLIAMSON

That's very fortunate seeing that I am the beloved wife of a great Churchwarden and a most important Synodsman.

MR WILLIAMSON

You seem to like better a talk with an ignorant labourer.

MRS WILLIAMSON

Please remember my dear love that I will talk to anybody that I like; that I will never ask your permission first; that I don't care a straw whether you are vexed or pleased; that your opinion on what I do or say is the least thing in the world to me; that I certainly would rather talk to any body but you; that as the most miserable day of my life was when I married you so the happiest day of my life will be when I bury you; that—

MR WILLIAMSON
(*Raising his voice*)
Shut up. Shut up; by God it's a living death to live with you. Get out of my sight for God's sake.

MRS WILLIAMSON
(*Speaking very loudly*)
When I like Mr W. when I like; don't shout at me; don't think it's the men in the works you're bullying; don't think I'm afraid of you; don't—
(*The door on [blank] opens suddenly, and Clarice rushes in excitedly, talking rapidly as she enters.*)

CLARICE
Da, Mother, here's Mr Bishopson; he wants to speak to you about the Harvest Festival; and he has asked me to go down and help him decorate the church—with flowers and fruit you know—here he is —come along Mr Bishopson; you'll let me go won't you, mother —and I can bring down the flowers you bought today for the Church—Da, did you get the apples and things you promised?
(*During this outburst the Reverend Anthony Bishopson, B.A., curate of St Denis' has entered, and has timidly shaken hands with Mr and Mrs Williamson. He is a young man of about thirty years, very pale and very thin. He is apparently nervous and embarrased, and stand[s] mutely by while Clarice continues to speak.*)

CLARICE
Sit down, do Mr Bishopson; you really must have a cup of tea with us before we go down to the Church; mustn't he mother.

MRS WILLIAMSON

Oh! of course he will dear. I'm sure, Mr Bishopson, we will have a great congregation at the Harvest Festival.

MR BISHOPSON

Surely, Mrs Williamson. The Bishop is certain to attract a great crowd. It is very good of him to come, don't you think so?

MRS WILLIAMSON

It is his duty Mr Bishopson; in God's eyes a Bishop is no more than I am. Indeed, I don't think Bishops are at all necessary to the spread of the Gospel.

CLARICE

Don't talk nonsense, mother; how can you know as much about the Church's needs as Mr Bishopson?

MRS WILLIAMSON
(*Severely*)
I'm not talking nonsense, Clarice; please to remember that I'm your mother, and that I read my Bible as well as Mr Bishopson, or any Bishop.

MR WILLIAMSON

I'm glad to say that the subscriptions are coming in splendidly towards the Susentation Fund. We have now upwards of fifty pounds. That's very good, isn't it? Where did you put the book that the names are in, my dear?
(*Mrs W. hurries over to the piano stool, and from underneath a pile of music, she takes a book, which she gives to Mr W.*)

MRS WILLIAMSON

There dear, I put it under the music for safety.

MR WILLIAMSON

How thoughtful of you, dear; I'll have some more subscriptions to enter, Mr Bishopson, & then I'll join you. And you, dear, please get the tea for I'm sure, Mr Bishopson will be delighted to take a cup with us. (*Exit*)

MR BISHOPSON

Really Mr Williamson, you are too kind; really, you must not give Mrs Williamson so much trouble; really—

CLARICE

Nonsense Mr Bishopson; it's no trouble, sure it's not ma?

MRS WILLIAMSON

Not the slightest dear; it will be delightful to have Mr Bishopson with us to tea; play something for him while I look after the things —she plays beautifully Mr Bishopson.

MR BISHOPSON

Really; how surprising—I mean of course, that I'm sure she does; it will be a great pleasure, really, Miss Clarice to listen to you.

MRS WILLIAMSON

(*Archly to Mr Bishopson*)

Take care of her till tea is ready, Mr Bishopson.

MR BISHOPSON

I will, really with pleasure. (*Exit Mrs W.*)

(*Clarice goes over and stands before the fire, looking at the hearthstone that Joe has tiled.*)

CLARICE

The tiles looks lovely really, don't they, Mr Bishopson?

MR BISHOPSON

(*Going over and standing at the opposite side of the fireplace*)

They do indeed; they are really quite beautiful.

CLARICE

They make the room look very nice, don't they?

MR BISHOPSON

Really, very nice indeed. (*A pause.*)

MR BISHOPSON

Excuse me, Miss Clarice, but that is really a lovely rose you are wearing.

CLARICE

Isn't it? A beautiful shade of pink.

MR BISHOPSON
It really suits your beautiful complexion, admirably.

CLARICE
(*Coyly*)
Oh! Mr Bishopson.

MR BISHOPSON
Pardon me, Miss Clarice; I really meant no harm, you know. I'm afraid I spoke without thinking. (*A pause.*)

MR BISHOPSON
Will you play something for me dear Miss Clar—Williamson; I should really like to hear you sing— I do really love to hear you singing in the choir—I

MISS CLARICE
And *I* do love to hear you preaching, Mr Bishopson.

MR BISHOPSON
Really, it is exceedingly good of you to say that—

CLARICE
(*Rapidly*)
Oh! Yes, I feel so curious when you preach that I hardly hear a word you say.

MR BISHOPSON
(*A little fearful*)
Dear me; will you please play something.

CLARICE
(*Going over to the piano, Bishopson following*)
And what shall I play? (*archly*) would you like a love-song?

MR BISHOPSON
(*Again afraid*)
Well, really, I think I'd prefer a hymn—Onward Christian Soldiers, or something like that, you know.

CLARICE
(*Disappointed*)
Oh! I don't like hymns; besides this isn't Sunday.

MR BISHOPSON
All days are the same, or ought to be, to the true Christian, aren't they, dear—ar—Miss Clarice?

CLARICE
Oh, Mr Bishopson. I'm surprised to hear a good Protestant say such a thing. "Remember to keep holy the Sabbath day." Surely, we do things on week days we would never think of doing on Sundays. At least, I think so.

MR BISHOPSON
Oh! indeed you're right, Miss Clarice; the Sabbath is indeed a day of rest and gladness a day of joy and light; a balm of care and sadness, most beautiful most—

CLARICE
Did you ever hear this, Mr Bishopson, The Heart's Welcome to Love? Oh! it's an awfully beautiful air.

MR BISHOPSON
No, never. Please play and sing it for me.
(*During this conversation, Jim has entered by door on [blank]; he has taken a sweeping brush, and leaning on the handle, he watches the pair beside the piano, with a broad smile in his face.*)

CLARICE
(*Suddenly*)
Were you ever in love, Mr Bishopson?

MR BISHOPSON
(*Confounded*)
Never, Clarice, never! That is I was never in love really—till now. (*Losing himself*) But my heart has welcomed love at last. It enshrines a beautiful, lovely, fair, gentle little creature.

CLARICE
(*Shyly*)
And who is she, Mr Bishopson, may I ask.

MR BISHOPSON
Call me Benjamin. Please, Clarice, it would give me joy abounding, really.

CLARICE
(*Slowly, & looking at him roguishly*)
May I ask if I know her.

MR BISHOPSON
You may (*he bends down towards her—she is sitting on the piano stool playing idly—as if to kiss her*).

JIM
Be careful, be careful; mind what you do.
(*Clarice and Bishopson start away from each other, very much frightened. Clarice busies herself by quickly looking through the music and Bishopson stands awkwardly looking at Jim.*)

JIM
You were in a dangerous position that time friend; it was well I come to your rescue.

MR BISHOPSON
I was discussing music with Miss Williamson; and—really, what do you want here;

JIM
Just come up for the brush. Wasn't it providential?

MR BISHOPSON
Who is this fellow, Miss Williamson?

CLARICE
One of my father's workmen; they're doing something to the kitchen range: please do not talk to him.

MR BISHOPSON

Well, now that you've got the brush, you'd better go; this is no place for you. And remember the next time you come into a room —a room devoted to the private use of a family that you are to knock so that those who occupy it may determine whether you are to enter or no. Do you understand?

[JIM]

Of course; but bein' workin' here a few minutes ago, & nobody bein' in it, when I come back I thought it would be just as empty an' never imagined that you was here acourtin' of the young lady.

MR BISHOPSON

Pardon me saying you are very presumptuous & equally impertinent, and I certainly shall complain about insolent temerity to Mr Williamson.

[JIM]

I hope you won't do that on me sir; I didn't mean to come in on you sudden like; I wasn't thinkin' of anything only the brush, & it wasn't my fault you and the young lady was—

MR BISHOPSON

We were discussing music, as I told you before, a theme probably about which you know nothing. Drink would probably be more congenial to you.

[JIM]

I like an odd pint sir, right enough; I'll not deny it; oh! no I'm no hypocrite, but I hope I don't go too far with it, never. As for music, I like it well; an' not that I wants to boast sir, or blow me own horn, down where I live, all me butties 'ill allow that I'm a topper at a mouth organ or a tin whistle. An' if we're here workin' tomorro, an' you an' the young lady's agreeable, I'll be delighted to play you a waltz—The Dream of Love a beautiful one—or if yous 'ill rather have a reel or jig, I'll give you the "Lass o' Killeekrankee or Haste to the Weddin'."

83

[JOE]
(*Shouting outside*)
Are you comin' with that bloody brush?

[JIM]
(*Running to the door and shouting savagely*)
Take your bloody time, will you—d'ye think I am a kind of a La-
bour Mercury with wings growin' out o' me heels.

MR BISHOPSON
(*Runs over gets the sweeping brush, thrusts it into [Jim's] hand seizes
him by the shoulder, shoves him out through the door, which he closes
with a bang, saying*)
Get out immediately, sir, how dare you use such a horribly vulgar
and profane expression before a young lady. Get out at once, &
never come back here again. (*To Clarice—*) These are the kind of
ruffians that are looking for their rights, and shouting that they are
as good as we. The impudence, the vulgarity the profanity the ignorance of these low-class herd are almost enough to compel one
to become convinced that there is nothing to be done but to de-
prive them of all opportunity of coming into contact with decent
and respectable people. I hope my dear Miss Williamson, that you
are not frightened, and that you did not hear that fellow's vile and
vulgar expressions.

CLARICE
(*Archly*)
How could I be frightened and you with me? But he is a very low
fellow isn't he, Mr Bishopson? And the horrible language he used,
too. It would be terrible to have to listen to him for long. And
what must the others be when he's such a horrid fellow.

MR BISHOPSON
The others! Why I suppose they're all alike; what difference can
there be between him and his other associates or oh! what's this
he called them.

84

CLARICE

His "butties."

MR BISHOPSON

What a horrid ugly vulgar word really. I suppose it means something dreadful.

CLARICE

It must of course. And yet the Rector thinks a terrible lot of that horrid fellow.

MR BISHOPSON

The Rector! Surely, the Rector has nothing to do with that man.

CLARICE

Oh! if you had come to the Parish six months ago you'd know all about it. The Rector could do nothing without [Jim]. He was his right hand man, and the white haired boy of the Parish. You couldn't say a word against him—though I never liked him for I well knew the sort he was and so does father.

MR BISHOPSON

And your dear mother, too, of course.

CLARICE

Mother doesn't know him: it's only lately she attends church. She belongs to the Plymouth Brethren & has curious notions about Conversion, Salvation & other things like that.

MR BISHOPSON

This fellow lives in the Parish still then.

CLARICE

Oh yes: with his sister in some room in [blank] Street.

MR BISHOPSON

And what was it induced him to leave the Church, particularly when he was such a great friend of the Rector's.

CLARICE

I'm sure I don't know, I take no interest in him; he is very little loss to the Church, I'm sure; but I heard my father say that he is a Labour agitator or something, & says the Church always takes the part of the employers against the men.

MR BISHOPSON

Striving for the meat that perisheth, & will probably die in his sin.

CLARICE

Let us talk of something else Mr Bishopson. Would you like me to play that piece now for you.

MR BISHOPSON

(*Looking at his watch*)

Dear me I never imagined Time flew so fast. I shall be compelled I'm afraid, to postpone that delicious pleasure. The Vestry will meet in half an hour to make final arrangements for the Harvest Festival; besides the church decoration hasn't even been commenced yet. Really Miss Williamson I shall have to postpone that delicious pleasure. Indeed I fear that I cannot even wait for tea. I—

CLARICE

Oh! Mr Bishopson and you promised to wait!

MR BISHOPSON

I did Miss Clarice, but I nearly forgot about the meeting & the Church Decoration and you don't know the sort of man the old Rector is, one of the old school you know—thinks we should regard nothing but our duties, & thinks of nothing but carrying out of his orders. It is really shameful that such an old man should continue to be Rector of a Parish. I really don't know what the Bishop can be thinking of. I wonder could I see Mr Williamson for a few moments before I go.

[manuscript of unfinished revision of Act I breaks off at the end of the page]

Transcriber's Note

Sean O'Casey's as yet unproduced earliest extant play is here published for the first time. We have had almost no difficulty in transcribing the sole surviving manuscript, now in the New York Public Library's Berg Collection of English and American Literature, and much pleasure in the discovery of matters of considerable dramatic and biographical interest. "The Harvest Festival" is a rich melodrama of class struggle, with ironically pointed clashes among representatives of Church, Employer, and Labour, and with hymns to the Irish Mother—and Son: bright nuggets of remembered or transformed early life. It is hard to see why the Abbey Theatre, with its roster of players perfect for the leading parts, could not have worked with the emerging playwright on an exciting production. Perhaps too exciting for Yeats and the other directors in that volatile time—one can imagine their horror at the thought of staging some of the "nice talk" of violence and workers' bravado.

Except in the stage directions, punctuation has been changed only minimally (quotation marks, periods after abbreviations, apostrophes in contractions) and no spelling has been altered that might be dialectal. In short the dialogue has been kept free of editorial conjectures that might misrepresent O'Casey's approximations of the spoken word or his differentiations of characters by their sentence rhythms. The rare slip of the pen which he immediately corrected is not included in the transcription, nor the accidental repeating of a word at the start of a new line. Editorial insertions absolutely needed to make sense are printed within square brackets. O'Casey's significant revisions are given in brief textual notes in the Appendix, for the reader interested in the author's stops and starts; also minor editorial emendations. In these notes the words and punctuation deleted by O'Casey are printed in italic within square brackets, his insertions in roman type within angle brackets: numbers refer to pages and lines of the printed text.

An incomplete revision of the first act, which was kept with the original manuscript, is included in the Appendix, to show the direction in which O'Casey might have gone had he chosen to revise the entire play. It is in a less finished state than the original first act, and since it does not seem to blend with the original second and third acts nor appear to have been intended to go with them it could not suitably replace the original text for any playing version.

The New York Public Library   W.L.C.
Autumn 1978

Notes, Revisions, and Emendations

See Transcriber's Note, p 87 above

2.1 Cast] ms: Caste. Probably a slip of the pen, but it could be an appropriate socialist joke.

2.21 Ō Cathasaigh] Gaelic form of O'Casey's name, that he used since 1906.

2.22 18, Abercorn Road.] O'Casey's home address from 1897 until he moved in 1920, his mother having died in late 1918. Shaw wrote him here in December 1919.

3.22 Bible.] ms: [*b*] ⟨B⟩ible, [*which is almost concealed by a collection of huge cabbages, huge potatoes, huger turnips and other vegetables.*]

3.30 work.] ms: work [*and is ... right. ...*]—the bottom of the sheet (Act 1, ms p 1) is torn off here with a trace of cancelled stage direction remaining. P 2 continues without a gap in sense.

4.5 affected] ms: effected

4.9 in thin . . . tones] mended from: in a thin . . . tone

5.8 Begor] mended from: Begod

5.22 themselves look as] ms: themselves [*as*] ⟨look as⟩

5.33 came to] ms: came to [*this*]

7.4 Mrs Williamson] ms: [*Tom*] Mrs. Williamson

7.17 that's going] ms: that go[*es*] ⟨ing⟩

8.31 talk of why] ms: talk of [*the*] why

8.34 couldn't] ms: [*couldt*] couldn't

9.7 we stop] ms: we [*try*] stop

9.9 anything he] ms, perhaps: anything that he (word deleted by ink blot)

9.32 Labour Leaders] ms: [*employers*] ⟨Labour Leaders⟩

10.8 kill you or] ms: kill you [*an*] or

11.20 Just about as] ms: Just ⟨about⟩ as

12.2 (Bishopson is] ms: preceded by cancelled: [*They are certainly be*] (i.e. beauties; see below)

13.4 Mrs Williamson] ms: [*Jack*] Mrs. Williamson

13.21 miserable] ms: [*happy*] ⟨miserable⟩

15.14 deal less . . . than I] ms: deal [*than*] less . . . than [*me*] ⟨I⟩.

15.26 workers] ms: [*working*] workers

16.3 listen to him] ms: [*listen to him*] hear him

16.9 forces] ms: [*sho*] forces (start for "shows"?)

18.6 Bishopson] ms: [*Williams*] Bishopson

18.7 left] ms: [*back*] ⟨left⟩

18.26 wait] ms: [*well a*] ⟨wait⟩

19.6 white shirts] ms: which shirt

21.18 see you here] ms: see you hear

22.11 He draws] ⟨conjectural⟩ ms: He das? / has?

26.22 sharp and active.] ms: [*quick*] sharp and active.

28.8 I['m] never [out] ms: ?ault, or possibly: out

28.25 ever come to Church] ms: ⟨ever⟩ come [*ever*] to Church

28.30 an says] ms: as says

30.3 An' those] ms: An' the those

30.4 sidesmen] ms: [*side*⟨s⟩*men*] sidesmen

31.21 right, at which] ms: right, ⟨at⟩ which

32.21 to know John] perhaps a slip for: to know you, John; ms: to know, John

33.13 you liked my] ms: you my

34.11 am too strong] ms: am strong

36.3 that John knows] ms: that knows (but the conjectural insertion seems clearly required.)

39.15 hymns for me, for] ms: hymns for, for

39.18 after a while when] ms: after a while [*after*] when

43.16 Jack:] ms: [*The Rector:*] Jack:

45.26 Bill?] ms: [*Jack*] Bill?

45.31 who is] ms: [*who was*] who is

46.15 all young children] ms: all [*child*] young children

46.17 provide for] ms: provide [*the*] for

48.31 whether] ms: [*and*] whether

49.22 are protesting] ms: protesting

51.6 Williamson] ms: Mr. Bishopson (an obvious error)

53.5 we were all as] ms: we all as

54.3 meet place in which] ms: meet ⟨place in which⟩

54.17 Bishopson] ms: [*Williamson*] Bishopson

54.31 his word] ms: [*your*] ⟨his⟩

55.11 I'm almost] ms: I almost

56.23 Hymns or] ms: Hymns [*of*] or

58.7 him self] possibly mended to: him Self

58.17 liveliest respect] ms: liveliest

58.27 shot Rocliffe] ms: shot [*him*] ⟨Rocliffe⟩

60.21 enough] Preceded by a short cancelled word.

60.21 me and Clarice home.] ms: me [*home.*] ⟨and Clarice home.⟩

62.6 bury him an'] ms: bury an'

62.9 The Rector:] ms: [*Mr.*] The Rector:

62.27 and even] ms: and [*if*] even

62.27 would probably] ms: would [*have*] probably

63.12 church in] ms: church [*of*] ⟨in⟩

64.4 Bill: So you're] ms: Bill: [*I was thinkin' this 'ud be the way*] So you're

67.5 sense of] ms: sense of [*the*]

67.26 Tom] There is a space after "Tom" for a last name or a new name for the character Tom Nimmo of the original version: "Joe" was the name O'Casey eventually chose (75.30). We have used "Tom" as written until the name change. See also note to 84.1.

67.26 in the hearth] ms: in [*a*] ⟨the⟩ hearth

67.28 [Jim] who has] There is a space for a new name of the character Jack Rocliffe of the original—O'Casey finally decided upon "Jim" (72.19 and 20). For easier reading, "[Jim]" will be printed in place of the spaces or dashes O'Casey used at first. A new last name "Driscoll" is used (70.3). See also note to 83.7.

68.14 passage,] ms: passage, [*leaves the*] ⟨replaces the⟩

69.10 brickie] An ink blot obscures the end of the word, which we retrieve from the original version.

69.27 *Jim*] ms: Jack

69.30 exercise.] Following this sentence O'Casey began a new page (Act 1, p 3) describing Williamson at length, marked for deletion by a jagged line up to the point of the closing bracket in the transcription which follows. The two sentences after this are an implied deletion since they do not continue the sense of the stage direction without the deleted material. O'Casey may have planned to revise only the actually deleted matter but the text reads more clearly by putting the whole passage here:

[*As a Foreman* [of] *in the engineering works of a large company he is possessed of a dignity that is ludicrous, vulgar and pompous, and which, frequently, expresses itself in a half-savage domineering attitude towards others. He is destitute of any idea outside of the intelligence he has acquired by long practice that is necessary to carry out the duties his position demands from him. As churchwarden of the Parish of St Denis, which honour has been conferred upon him by the parishioners at the last parochial elections—his dignity has expanded into a fuller importance. He demonstrates this lively sense of increased importance by adding numerous pendants to his watchchain; by the adornment of one of his fingers by a heavy gold ring containing a large red stone; by wearing a suit of the latest fashion, & by adopting a toilet of ties and white shirt in which he is essentially uncomfortable. He has a large, wide, heavy face; a vulgar mouth, a high forehead, caused, not by thought or study, but by the disappearance of hair on the front part of his head. He parades his pompous nature when talking to anyone whom he thinks occupies a station inferior to his own, and has a shifty and uneasy demeanour when speaking to those who are mentally above him, or who have a moral courage greater than his own. He seems to imagine that, by securing election to the position of Churchwarden, he has inalienably acquired the prerogative to a seat in the Senate of Heaven;* [of being] *that he is an infallible* [blank] *of the morals & virtues of others while being himself immune from the criticism of all. He no longer measures things by the connection of the Church with himself; but measures all things by the connection of himself with the Church. His vanity and importance have elevated him to the position of one of Christ's patrons. He goes to Church, not because he feels any necessity for such a course of conduct, but because he thinks it essential for the good of others that he should be there.*] He is astounded at the idea of any parishioner being absent when he deigns to be present. His name appears in the subscription lists of the various Parochial Funds, for he argues, if you cannot purchase Paradise, you certainly ought to have a few shares in the company that runs the business.

70.23 Susentation] *Mispronunciation of* sustenation. See also 78.21.

71.12 I'm not] ms: I'm [*in*] no

72.4 *Jim*] ms: Jack

Note: p 72ff. From here on the names of Mr & Mrs Williamson are almost never spelled out; so we retain the ms abbreviations.

72.25 earth, earthy] ms: earth[*y*], earthy

72.26 happen to me] ms: happen to me [*now is n*]

72.27 than] ms: that

74.32 believer.] ms: believer. [*Jim*]

77.1 that your] ms: that [*I*]⟨your⟩

83.7 (and below) Jim:] ms: Joe. O'Casey started a new page in the ms here, continuing the scene of Jim's interruption of the lovers. He might have decided to have the interruption be by Joe (and not gone back to change the introductory comments of "Jim") or he might have been changing the name of the Jack/Jim character again. More likely, though, he had forgotten, in the interim since the workers' last appearance (76.4–7), that it was Tom's name he had changed to Joe. In any case, the scene sounds more like Jim's codding the lovers with a Joe-like pose.

83.21 probably be] ms: be [line break] probably be

84.1 (and below) Joe:] ms: Tom. See note to 83.7.

85.26 some room] ms: a some room